Pocket Money

Matata Muthoka

Pocket Money
ISBN: 978-1499633474

P. O. Box 2981 – 20100 Nakuru
Tel: +254 731187075
Mobile: 0721137478

Content

Introduction _5

Chapter 1: Money Demystified _9

Chapter 2: Early Lessons On Money_ _ _ _ _ _ _ _ _ _ _ _ _ _ _ _ _29

Chapter 3: The Missing Links _51

Chapter: 4 The Power Of Intention _ _ _ _ _ _ _ _ _ _ _ _ _ _ _ _ _77

Chapter: 5 Money And Life Choices _ _ _ _ _ _ _ _ _ _ _ _ _ _ _95

Chapter 6 The Pocket Money Equation (Income Equation)_ _ _103

Chapter 7: Y- Income _105

Chapter 8: Consumption Of Pocket Money_ _ _ _ _ _ _ _ _ _ _117

Chapter 9: Savings And Pocket Money_ _ _ _ _ _ _ _ _ _ _ _ _121

Chapter 10: Taxes_ _125

Chapter 11: Investment (I) _129

Chapter 12: Case Studies _133

Chapter 13: Tracking Your Pocket Money_ _ _ _ _ _ _ _ _ _ _159

Conclusion _167

To my parents Loise Mutete
and Benson Muthoka

Acknowledgement

Much gratitude goes to an unknown girl whom I met in a supermarket with her mum. As she walked with her mother she continuously requested to load the tray with any item that interested her. The girl's mother's response was a continuous "impulse buying" every time the girl wanted something. Listening to this conversation I thought of what the girl's mother was imprinting in the child's mind.

I thought of a guide that can be of help to parents as they introduce their children to money. I walked to the bookshelf but I could not find a suitable book. I went to several book stores but I did not find any. It was then that I thought of writing a book on children and money.

This book is a product of inspiration from that girl whom I do not know but who was seeking for direction. It is my hope that it can be of help to many people out there. I would also wish to thank all those who have given their ideas, edited and criticised it.

May the almighty God richly bless you all

Introduction

It's about 10.00pm immediately after study preps; like bees in the twilight hours of the day, we retreat to our dormitories.

Once in our cubicles, the dormitory captain summons us in a din like tone at the main dormitory entrance. We immediately move to the said direction. We find the school captain, dormitory captain and other prefects and soon gather around them.

The dormitory captain called the meeting to order by switching off the lights then putting them back on. Angrily, he announced that amongst us we had thieves who stole money, shoes, clothes, underwear, plates, and spoons among other things. On this particular occasion, he said that a form four student had lost 30,000 shillings. The boy was called to explain the miraculous disappearance of his money from his safe.

"I had left money in my box inside my old shoes. The box had a padlock by the name "Extra Top Security," the boy called Pato explained. The boy in question reported that on coming back from games at around six, he found that the box was closed like it usually was. The padlock had not been broken but the money had moved out of the box through osmosis or diffusion, some 'jini' had crept in and out with the money or worse still somebody had the key to the box if not a master key.

We all listened to the narration keenly. A thorough inspection was immediately conducted but they could not trace the cash. With no cash being found, the prefects crafted a plan to scare the culprit. One of the prefects took off his dirty inner wear, produced a new King James Version Bible and Golden Bells hymn book then arranged them. We were then ordered to first skip the golden bells, then the bible and finally hold the smelly underwear while saying, "I did not steal the money and I am not a thief." This was happening as every one of us got into the dormitory from outside.

We did this but no one was caught. There was no suspect yet. The usual crooks in school residing in our dormitory faced it rough with kicks, slaps, punches and neck squeezing. These 'culprits' were tortured for many hours till late in the night but still no sign of mens rea.

We woke up the following morning for dawn preps at 5.00am as usual. The preps went on smoothly till six and some of us who were involved in sporting activities headed for practice. We spent like an hour every morning practicing with our games tutor. At the same time those who were not engaged in sports were meant to come back for classes by 6.40am meaning no one was to be found in the dormitories.

On this fateful day, one of the volley ball players was sent to pick a wire to tighten up a weak volleyball net. The particular student had volunteered saying he had a wire in the sleeping quarters. On arriving at the dormitory, Kaura found the door locked from the inside. He instantly became nervous and curious. He tiptoed and peeped through the slim window pane not covered by the curtains. He saw the dormitory captain in his friend's cubicle. The captain had opened his friend's wooden box. Kaura observed this for about three minutes as he tried to hold his breath but his heart beat soared higher. Here was a keeper stealing money from his students' boxes. Here was a shepherd suckling the mother sheep and starving the lambs.

Pocket Money

Pocket money can be said to be money given or earned which is meant to take care of petty expenses. The word is popular with school going children who are given money by their care givers in anticipation of unexpected mishaps and needy situations that warranty spending. This money is not audited like it happens in corporate circles. However, this subject is rarely discussed and is normally pushed under the carpet in many families.

CHAPTER 1

MONEY
DYMYSTIFIED

Pocket Money

Istop suddenly in one of the busy streets of Nairobi and decide to have a break. Before I sit, I fight the great urge to continue with my endless journey but finally halt at a bench. I observe people of all ages rush here and there in all directions. Pedestrians on the streets were stepping on each other, not saying 'sorry', thanks to the forgotten etiquette. People's shirts and sweaters had weakened near the shoulders, while their shoes had bent sideways at the heels out of friction with the black tar.

Many of the people I saw had brown A4 or A5 envelopes, hand bags, keys, ink pens. It seemed all the people had one mission in their mind for the day- to make a kill. Make an extra coin. It is absurd that all these people had been to school locally or abroad, gone through the 8-4-4, 7-4-2-3 or are products of some other system out there. As I sit there I wonder what these diverse education systems prepare people for in life. Spend? Save? Invest? If so, what are they rushing to do, save or make?

If you try to ask any of these people what they are after, they will consider you lunatic. If you are lucky, you may get an answer like, *"masaa ni pesa"* or *"masaa ni mbesha"* or "time is money". Generation after generation use this saying as it has existed in the longest time possible. However, have you ever stopped and asked yourself, "What is money?" For those who were lucky it might have been defined in a business class as a medium of exchange.

As I sit on that City Council of Nairobi –CCN– branded chair I ponder over these questions:-
• What is money?
• How is it earned?
• Is the way it is earned the only way?
• What can it do?

- Is there a formula for getting more money than other people?
- How did I learn about what I know about money?
- Who owns these cars, lorries, public vehicles, the road, the tall sky scrapers including the railway and the aeroplanes screaming in the sky?
- How did those who own these things come to own them?
- Is it possible? If it is? How is it possible?

These questions linger on in my mind and I wonder if it is possible for all of us to stop and think of the same. It is ridiculous that we have so much in the education system but actually very little about the practicalities of how to generate money. You have a lot, you buy a lot, you have little and your chances of making it big are limited.

I sometimes wish we could have one lesson known as 'money' and learn it the way we learn Kiswahili, English and Mathematics to answer the above questions. However, unless we change the education system to accommodate these changes we only learn to infer implicitly from the environment. This book tries to fill the missing links that condemn some people to poverty and others to colossal richness.

Defining Money
The Oxford Dictionary defines money as the means of paying for something or buying something. Macmillan English Dictionary defines the word money as what you earn, save, invest and use to pay for goods and services. A further explanation of what money is by the dictionary says that money is the "means" that allows you to survive. This denotes that money is a way or a method of facilitating one's living.

Pocket Money

In the above definition, the word money means a medium of exchange. This means that money exchanges hands with something else. Money is not limited to coins, notes and cheques; in fact money is anything that can serve the purpose of a medium of exchange. The history of money dates back to when people could exchange goods for goods or goods for services. Money was developed from gold, silver and cowrie shells standard in different parts of the world to the centre holed coins. It then evolved to notes, to cheques, to cards and then electric money systems.

Today, we do not have to carry money in form of coins, notes or even cheque books to carry out any transactions. All we have to do is deal with electronic numbers in our phones and computers. A simple example of this is the transfer of money from the bank via phone to settle debts. In this case no cash or paper is needed but still money has changed hands. What really happens is that electronic numbers have decreased in the bank, increased in the account holder's phone, and then decreased again when one pays the bills causing an increase in electric figures in the recipients account. What works is the belief that the numbers that feature represent worthiness and value.

In such a scenario, no money has changed hands but those involved are satisfied. Jonathan Self, in his book The Teenagers Guide To Money (2007 pg. 27-28) says, "It is not what is made from but what it represents that makes it valuable."
Money represents time and effort spent by the bearer of what is generally agreed as money. The time and effort is what we refer to as labor. That is why it varies and is quantified depending on the level and type of skill put in use.

A person wakes up early at 5.00am drives or is driven to work by public means or packs himself in a full train on a muddy day. Some people work from 8.00am to 4.00pm while others spend over 24hours at work; policemen spend most hours manning others and their property. A few others work with the belief that their effort and time offered when quantified will be paid in form of salaries or wages.

Whether what will be paid will be in form of coins, notes and cheques or in electronic numbers, increase in their bank accounts or a pile of goods is what settles the debt. Therefore, it is not what it is but what it represents. What is involved are numbers. It is our belief in what we call money that makes it work.

This is the belief that a certain amount of coins compensates for my time and efforts, the belief that Mpesa, Zap, Yu cash or Orange money numbers in my phone represent compensation of efforts and time that I spent. This belief breeds the confidence in any money system that makes it work.

It is important that everyone understands the basics of money at an early age. It is rather unfortunate that money is what matters most in the modern world. Money should not be made a dominant factor in any school or education system. In our learning institutions we have subjects that prepare the students for life, agriculture, electricity, economics, law, biology, chemistry among others. What we are not told is that these are professions or tools which we should use to make money. To me, these are tools which facilitate the acquisition of money which makes people tick.

Education systems teach people limited options of making money for various reasons. Some of the reasons are politically instigated to keep the masses dependent on their professions in order to make a living thus enabling the government to survive. The government requires man power hence the vital professions of medicine, teaching, farming, fishing, engineering and many more areas of expertise which are required in every country. Becoming a professional provides one with enough to survive but not a lot of wealth.

The rich in the society have soared limitedly in their careers and enormously in financial intelligence. They have mastered the art of using the fooled intellectuals to make money. Saying this reminds me of a story by a close friend by the name Regina.

One day as Regina drove from one job to another; her Toyota 110 model car was hit by a ruthless *matatu* in the streets of Nairobi. She became so furious that the *matatu* owner had to cut short his myriad errands and join her at the scene. When he came he looked at her and at the vehicle, he chuckled. His words stirred harsher and sharpened emotions in Regina. The *matatu* owner agreed to repair the car after the police intervened. As the Toyota 110 wreck was being pulled to his garage, he offered to travel with Regina in his brand new Prado. As they drove towards Githurai where his garage was situated, a venomous Regina asked Masuri, the Matatu owner, why he said her vehicle was bought via a loan.

Mr. Masuri offered to explain what he called 'the predicament' of the intellectuals. Masuri asked Regina what she did for a living and she proudly explained that she had two jobs. Regina worked with the Higher Education's Loans Board and also with the Kenya Power and Lighting Company. She was also a part time student at the same time. On hearing these words Masuri replied, "I knew from the beginning that you are an intellectual and probably this vehicle is bought through a loan you are repaying or you just finished paying."

The words flowing from Masuri angered Regina. At first she cursed inwardly the cruelty and rudeness of Masuri. She thought of how rich people monopolized and disliked the poor. It suddenly dawned on her that it is the poor intellectuals who dislike themselves for believing superficially and not thinking beyond their noses. According to Masuri, those who work for the rich are the intellectuals who do not know what to do with their superb skills.

Masuri said that in every education system, there are unconventional thinkers who run and own the conventional thinkers. There are pupils or students at every stage who follow through the system from day one to last day without failure and milk the conventional wisdom. The wisdom of grades provides food, house, water, money, health care, pleasure and comfort. They follow these systems dociled by their obedience to the systems that exist. This category of convectional thinkers end up being marvelous students, meticulous resume writers and forever proud employees in large companies.

On the other hand, a few unconventional thinkers in schools appear dumb, sometimes slow and deviate. They question the connection between Biology and food, Agriculture and money, Chemistry especially Avogadro's number with food on the table, pleasure and the good life they hope for. A few of this group of people cannot elevate the hidden truth or the postponed gratification and eventually drop out of school and follow the less traveled and dreaded option (s).

Others who are unconventional in their thought choose to remain in the system. They slowly cultivate uniqueness in thought and deed and cut a niche of their own in the skies and mountains of riches. These are guys who will be in class to be trained on how to do something with others but later will employ their classmates. This makes all the difference.

A classic example is that of students training to be teachers then one of them later starts a school and employs the others, Masuri emotionally implored.

Masuri continued chanting words conceded by Regina as intolerable and abusive of individual's personality, choice and profession and especially one of her academic level.

"How much do you earn from these two jobs?" Masuri enquired.

"That is personal," Regina replied with a sneer.

"That is your biggest problem! Personal! Personal! Even when it is a covered wound 'personal' you call it. I know what you earn is not a lot?" Masuri continued.

"Why do you think so?" Regina asked.

"First you have two jobs because one cannot support you. Is that right?" Masuri stated.

"Perhaps" Regina meekly retorted.

"Not perhaps it is true. Secondly, the two jobs you have are not yours, you are employed. Somebody is using you to make money," Masuri pointed.

"No, I like my job and I like what I do therefore am not being used as a tool. I usually earn what I deserve." Regina explained candidly then turned to face Masuri. All along they were not facing each other. They were only testing each other through their eye anus.

"I also know that you are back to school with the hope that your employer might increase your salary. You've never given thought why people should be in school, just following systems without stopping to question them, the government and how the universe works," Masuri explained.

These words infuriated Regina because Masuri was partly correct and partly wrong in her opinion. Masuri was right that by Regina doing a Diploma in Sales and Marketing on top of her Master in Education Technology, and Bachelor of Education Arts she hoped for a salary increment. In fact, she had calculated that the course was to cost her 100,000/=. If she was to get a salary increase of 10,000/= to 15,000/= the cost would be covered in one year and the rest would be profit.

On the other hand Masuri's morsel was misguided that she had not given thought to why she was in school. To Regina, she was correct because she was educated, schooled and learned. Indeed a scholar, how could a scholar be wrong? In Masuri's wisdom Regina was another victim of irrational convectional conventionalism. She was full of skills, experience, time and energy waiting to be used to make money. In fact, in making money Regina had no difference with the tools in use or in store waiting to be used or transferred for further use. Companies make tools for use by people to produce other products just in the same way employees are made for use by organizations, institutions and the governments to make money and produce many benefits besides rendering services.

The producers of tools are companies, organizations and government. The employees in every organization cannot use themselves unless they are used like the tools in the same company. The education system produces employees taught so well to obey and think that without them the country would collapse. Taught to like what they do, not what they earn or can earn. They are taught to care about what they do not, how it helps them and taught to follow unquestioningly.

Pocket Money

Organizations want to employ the best because they are not always the best. However, they become better by sapping the fine labor the market has to offer. Once their juice is dry the intellectuals are spit and as pukes they become bites for other struggling organizations. That is the fate of an intellectual professional. To guard against irrelevance they seek relevance by going back to school, attending seminars or reading books. This stop gap measure buys them time in one company.

As their discussion oozed to an end, Masuri told Regina "I am not as educated, schooled or learned as you are but I use people like you to do what I want. It's not that I usually do not go to school neither do I attend seminars and workshops but my reason isn't your reason. I go to choose and learn a trick." Masuri said these words as he handed Regina a new key for her new car.

My friend cried later as Masuri's words sank. On reflecting back on her life, she realized that she took orders without questioning, despite her rich educational background. She was a liability to the companies she worked for and not an asset since her contribution to the organization was always counted for in the expenses column. A thorough analysis of her own life showed how desperate she needed others and not how others needed her. She realized how soon she can be replaced in her work place since there were many other people striving to become better employees.

What Masuri referred to as the 'predicament of intellectuals' is all about becoming the best employee not the best employer. Many people go back to school to ensure that they can compete favorably in society but not because they want to learn more about business. Intellectuals exist to be used and that is the rule that the smart rich guys live by. When you see me trying to become a better employee, sack me when you see me outperforming myself in your work fire me for I have not learnt.

The rich hire the best for example the best lawyer, best counselors, best teachers for their children and self best doctors and best of all there is. The elite know they can get the best because they are not the best in those fields. The rich may let you be the best in the areas that facilitate living but they would not let you beat them in matters that anchor life - money matters. They know with money, they call the shots in any arena and that is all that matters to them.

Two high school boys started a discussion on money. One of the boys had an uncle who worked in Mombasa and had lots of money. Life in their home was oiled with all the luxuries but on the contrary they had no peace at all. Money had not brought them happiness but instead had become a source of conflict. To this boy money was not good. The boy shared how increase in income in his uncle's house caused sorrow instead of pleasure. He vowed never to be rich but only have enough to survive. This boy conditioned his mind to getting money to a certain level. Being comfortable with little and whenever he would have more in pocket money, he would spend the extra until he was left with the little he could handle.

The other boy came from a family which never discussed money openly. His family struggled but had learnt to save money. Then a high school student with five shillings note was adored and worshiped. Each of these boys went through high school, finished and left to make the best of their lives.

Twenty years later, these two chaps now men in their late thirties met again. The one who had a rich uncle had done his best and became a high school teacher. The other one who had done well now owned his own school. Upon meeting, the two men sought to reflect on their lives in a roadside café. The one who worked for the Teachers Service Commission (TSC) said, "I told you I will only work to earn enough to support myself. I don't need to make more. That is exactly what I am doing. I usually get a large salary but because I cannot handle it all, the government manages it partly through taxes, the NSSF manages it through deductions, the church manages it for me through tithes and alms and the *chamaa's* manages the other part until I get what I can handle. Look, I am healthy, I am clothed, I have a family and I have built a house in my inherited piece of land. What else could I ask for?" The teacher contented with his life cheerfully explained.

The school proprietor had tones of money, a fleet of *matatus* plying in various routes besides running his own school. He too rated himself as healthy, happy but not contented. He knew contentment takes a man nowhere since you end up settling for less than you can achieve.

These are two men who ran their lives based on plans they had laid down in their teens. They had discerned from their environment and made choices on their relationship with money. One had chosen to be a slave while the other had opted to become a master of money. One had chosen to become a master of a profession in order to earn a living while the other had chosen to master money in order to use the professionals to make more money.

This book is about widening the scope of information before us in order to make informed choices. It is about not making emotional decisions which yolk us to death. Many times we make decisions to the best of our knowledge. We fail to make the best of lives or go further in life because of limited information.

Deep down, Regina was aware that Masuri was right. She had bought the car from a loan from her membership SACCO. According to Masuri, she had done well but missed the bigger picture which was, you do not borrow to consume, you borrow to invest.

In his words, borrowing to purchase a personal car was one big mistake many people make. This is because loans do not come for free. Besides you always have to repay the principle plus the interest which grows exponentially. According to Masuri, the lenders always fail to tell the borrowers the growth rate wholly. They mean it operates on a reducing balance but still grows just like compound interest grows when you save.

When you think critically, Regina borrowed and bought a nice brand new car. The car was undergoing wear and tear and was not bringing back anything of much value to her. She could drive it to work, pay packing fee for a whole day and in the evening drive back home. Taking it to a taxi operation agency never came across her mind and looking at the cost side made Regina look stupid in the eyes of Masuri. His words felt like a thorn in her flesh. She was so much concerned on comfort and how she appeared in the eyes of others despite how much her lifestyle cost her.

In Masuri's wisdom, if one has to borrow money, do it to invest. This way they would be assured of driving the car they want without worrying of it being repossessed. Borrow and invest in a viable venture so that your venture will be the one to repay the loan in its entirety besides buying you a car.
This way those who borrow benefit but not when they buy a liability.

Robert Kiyosaki in his book Rich Dad Poor Dad (1995), points out that the poor and middle class spend their lives buying liabilities while the rich and wealthy buy assets all through. This is true so true when you look around in today's society. Young people learn borrowing habits from a young age. Students borrow money to buy a loaf of bread, a T-shirt, designer clothes, sport accessories while others look at what could benefit them more and go for it. They will borrow to buy books, geometrical sets, attend an educational symposium or buy a calculator. Others end up buying things which waste their time and money. For example, two students borrow money from colleagues. One buys a computer game, while the other buys a calculator. These two accessories have an effect on the performance of these two students. The one who buys a calculator uses it in calculations and passes his exams. The other one who buys a computer game realizes it requires new batteries and spends more money again to make it work. Then he spends most of the time playing games and not finishing assignments in time and it later affects his results negatively.

The habits we learn in our formative years serve to force in purchasing assets or liabilities. Consider purchasing a T.V, which can either be an entertainment facility or an educational one. One thing we have to know is that when we switch on a T.V, we spend many hours watching it. We watch soap operas, football, campaigns, and debates which makes investors and media people rich and ourselves poor because we do not do anything constructive.

My argument is that since we all have 24hrs; these people lure us in using most of our time as they make money. For instance, watching soccer wastes our creative time as the player, media owner and advertisers make money from us. Unless we are watching T.V for a purpose then we do not have to watch it. Watching it all the time is simply a waste of time.

Ben Carson's mother knew this early and restricted Carson and his brother to limited time to watch T.V. On the other hand, most of our children like it because it is also a nice instrument to reward or reinforce desirable behaviors or punish undesirable behaviors. Ben Carson became a renowned pediatrician while his brother became an engineer.

Most actors on the T.V act over time and as you watch their last series they are on the run recording another. This way they ensure you are glued to the screen as they make an extra dime from you. That goes the same to politicians and business people. While people are busy listening to what they had earlier said, they are sealing other business deals that only benefit them.

We may limit T.V. for our children but fail to control our addiction to it. Many of us worship television yet we are separated from the T.V by our chores or occupation. This is a poor habit which is rampant amongst the hustlers. It is impossible for you to switch programs off and wait for only the important ones. Most T.V channels are screaming for your attention using a combination of strategies to capture your perception through the senses. What we do not realize is that by watching too much of it we do not add value to ourselves.

We get jealous of those making money through their televised programs and products advertised. We know that these products do not just exist or happen they are products of particular companies owned by individuals like you and me. These companies need to make so much money out of you the viewer, so they find a way to have people watch and listen to them.

Pocket Money

You should not get trapped in the endless race of pictures that keep you expectant of the next episode while the rich are expectant of the next deal. The rich are looking for the most watched program to squeeze in their advertisement. This creates a need in you that necessitates your spending that increases their income. You should change this unrewarding behavior. Stop and think about the one who owns the T.V Company you are watching, who owns the handkerchief company you have in your purse, who owns the toothpaste you use. Ask yourself what trait is in these people that you do not have.

When you start becoming less comfortable with the answers you get out of your life, try not to get desperate. Analyze your life and figure out what you can do to become like the many people who have made it big in life or aim to be better than them.

I once shared a meal with one of my nephews. He had a social sciences question paper as an assignment. My nephew could not answer where the Maasai came from so he asked me. With answer options like the sky, valley, mountain and the like, based on my history I answered the sky. This sounded rather peculiar to him so he became more curious. He asked about the origins of other tribes like the Kamba, Kikuyu, Luos, Turkanas and Kalenjins. After giving many explanations, he finally asked where the whites come from.

Although I had no answer, I liked the young chap's inquisitive nature. I encouraged him to aim for more in life and he is becoming more intellectual because of his inquisitive nature. Do not be the kind of person who just uses a product; ask yourself what product you can introduce to the market. Do not just listen to what others say, choose to be listened to, do not just buy, opt to have your products bought and do not just simply read stories instead let your stories be read. Generally, do not choose to be a spectator, let others to be your audience, do not follow rules but instead set the rules yourself.

The Tea Bag

An anonymous writer once said that a person going through adversity is like a tea-bag;

One will never know what kind of flavour (character) is in the tea bag until it is placed in hot water.

"Behold, I have refined thee, but not with silver; I have chosen thee in the furnace of affliction," Isaiah 48:10.

A tea bag is a small bag with tea leaves inside that one puts in water to make tea. Tea generally is a refreshment drink. The tea making process, environment and ingredients can help us understand a few issues about work environment and workers.

In my explanation I would take tea bags to be the worker or people. A cup full of water cold or hot and stirring would be taken as the working environment. The worker has inherent potential just like the tea leaves in the tea bag. The environment exists to squeeze all from the worker just like the water saps color, smell and nutrients from a tea bag. Note that even whatever is left in the tea bag is wet and no longer in its original form.

If we immerse a tea bag in hot water the tea bag will slowly release its nutrients and color and smell to the hot water. The hot water works to weaken the bonds of these chemical substances easily hence dissolving in water. Working environments have a similar feature as hot water. Creating an environment suitable to weaken an individual talents and gifts for use within the company should be the sole responsibility of the organization. An organization that does not know how to get and use the talents of its employees lacks in character.

On the other hand if we immerse a tea bag in cold water and withhold stirring. Then it will still release its color, smell and nutrients to the water but at a slower rate. The reason for this is that the cold water does not have enough strength to weaken the bonds holding the tea bag content together. A person working in an environment which is not tailored to mint and squeeze the best from the worker then will have the worker unutilized and the organization underperforming. Just as the cold water leaves much in the tea bag unutilized, the ill prepared working environment leaves the workers juice soaked but not sucked.

Suppose in addition we put a tea bag in a cup of cold water then stir. The nutrients will be released a little bit higher than when not stirred. This shows that supervision which could be likened to stirring increases the grip of the squeezing hand on the tea bag (employee) hence releasing more amount of required qualities i.e. time, energy and mental resources.

Also if we have the initial consideration of hot water but now stirred. Then we end up with a concentrated drink. The favorable working conditions are favorable for the organization to get the best from the worker but not for the worker to enjoy. It is like duping a cow with fodder for the milkman to milk more. The worker's skills, experience, and time are fully warmed out of him or her. With continuous stirring the potency of the tea bag ceases just like worker productivity reduces over time.

On the other hand, a tea bag quickly releases its content when put in hot water and stirred. At this point the tea bag has no option other than releasing the nutrients. This way tea is made fast and the tea bag losses its potency as fast too. This causes it to be withdrawn from the boiling tea. Workers working in organizations whose precincts are earnestly horned to suck all from workers fast lose value and are forced out of the company. The organization is incessantly enhancing its ability to use workers to enhance its results. In fact the best manager is the one capable of getting the most from the environment with the workers no matter the means.

The organization when run as cold unstirred water then they operate inefficiently. This is because the tea bag still has some nutrients to release and color to add to the water. The organizations aim is to sap all worker capacity daily. Therefore, by the time the tea bag is withdrawn from the water it has nothing left. This also applies to workers, the aim is to benefit the organization to the fullest.

Organizations are built to operate efficiently and effectively. This means a worker as a resource is utilized fully before they are sidelined. Sometimes people may choose to share a tea bag. Have it used to make tea in several cups. As the tea bag is glad to share its diminishing resources as it acquires dampness from each cup of water. This dampness is referred to as experience.

In the same way careers of people are utilized in different organizations each company acquiring the worker hoping to benefit from their skills and talent. As tea bag is withdrawn and immersed from one cup to another it acquires dampness. By the time the tea bag is used in the fourth cup even with stirring and boiling the output tends to diminish to bear minimum.

In times of shortage the tea bag may be dried to regain some potency. Workers soon realize that their potency is whining and have to increase their ability to add value to their company or else seek somewhere where their dampness may be appreciated. To guard against this they tend to go back to school just as the tea bag is withdrawn and dried.

For organizations the water has to be kept boiling and continuously stirred to extract the best juice the worker has to offer. The tea bag that losses its value is soon replaced. That is why people study management courses, to learn how to achieve what they want through others. To the workers, the aim of every organization is to get results through you. If by adding more firewood more will be achieved from you then the employer would not mind and would stir till one relents. If the supervisor doesn't know how to get results from people they are also replaced.

Lastly the tea bag is made and used. In the same way employees are made for use in certain specific industries hence division of labor and specialization. The tea bag is only tailored to make tea in one cup of water even after stirring and a string is tied to it to ensure it is pulled out when not needed any more. Similarly, workers are trained for particular jobs. Hence teaching, finance, law, etc. The tea bag and its tea have more purposes other than brewing tea. The worker trained for a particular job does it and he is pulled out by retrenchment, fired, death or retired just like a tea bag. The string to pull you from the organization after your sap is over is always present.

Assess your position and reposition yourself accordingly. Being rich and prosperous in the society is always one sided. One side makes the other rich by assuming the elite are leading the way. It is your choice if you want to remain a pauper as you fatten heifers with your time and sweat.

CHAPTER TWO

EARLY LESSONS
ON MONEY

Pocket Money

I decided to visit Nairobi one Saturday afternoon so I briskly walked to the stage. The touts and *manambas* were busy baying for my fare as they pulled and shoved anyone into their *matatus*. The idea that not everyone at the bus stop was traveling seemed to be elusive to them. I moved aside and looked around as I tried to figure out which *matatu* was convenient. A *matatu* that could carry 14 people was charging 100/= to Nairobi while 36 and 48 capacity vehicles were charging between 70/= and 80/=. The touts loudly sang their prices, it would be thought they were in a choir competition.

I noticed that once one got in the *matatu* he or she is long forgotten and those standing outside are constantly pestered by the marketers of the different *matatus*. As I stood at the stage, five secondary school students approached to board the 36 sitter *matatu*. They peeped through the door and inquired on the price to Nairobi. One of them who appeared to know it all or the group leader said, "It's the discomfort vehicle."

Apparently, this type of vehicle only operates with money in mind. It capitalizes on all available space in it and how people will sit is the least of the owner's worries. The *matatu* economizes on seats that anyone who is tall –5'6'– would not sit properly. One is forced to endure and not enjoy the journey. The girl then turned to the others and said, "I'd rather pay more and sit comfortably." She then led her troop to a 10 sitter vehicle waiting further away where the fare was almost double the price.

Gauging from this particular incident, it is evident that high school students have the highest opportunity to start learning and educating themselves on money. One thing is clear though, most students are given 'pocket' money but do not know how their guardians struggle to get the money. A few may be aware of the hard economic times and empathize with the giver.

In this incident, the power of peer pressure played out so well. One girl expressed dislike for a particular *matatu* and turned away from it and the others blindly followed her.
The psychology of working in groups influences us to make decisions and do things that if we were alone we would not have made. This way, we sometimes spend more in fares, expensive drinks, expensive purchases, night outs than what we had initially budgeted for.

The game of success is rarely won by following shoals like fish or abiding by what groups do. Unless you are the leader, you are bound not to meet your targets if all you do is follow people around like baboons. Success is won when one stops to question the direction of motion and the outcome of a particular action. Being the best in life may mean being left without friends, being labeled as a loner or a rascal. However, if what you are doing makes sense to you then go for it. Be the kind of person who does something that is rational because you have thought about it.

Students spend more money to get to destinations they would have gone with less. Students who know what planning is would choose to save any amount of money at every opportunity. They would seek to exploit opportunities that bring them income. Students are always given money that they are not accountable for. If one uses this money well, they can easily invest in something productive. As parents we are good at giving our children money yet we do not teach them how to use it.

Pocket Money

Before giving money to your child, ask yourself the following questions:-
- Why should I give this child money?
- How much money should I give him?
- Is the child I am giving money responsible?
- Is giving money the only way out?
- How can I make my child more responsible with money?
- In what ways does my son or daughter use their pocket money?
- Am I responsible enough with money to teach or mentor my child?
- When a child asks for money, is giving the only solution?
- When a child asks for a gift, a toy or something is giving it to him/her the solution?
- Is giving a child money teaching them about earning, spending, saving and investing?
- Does the curriculum teach my child about money?
- Should I assume nature will teach my child what I cannot teach them?

Sometimes we are so engulfed in our work that we miss crucial opportunities to teach our children about money. Children are misled when they are given money but not told how to use it. It is said that human beings are self actualizing so they are self directed. Human beings are believed to know what they want and how to get it. This may not really apply to children who we are giving money since they do not know how to earn it. Assuming a child learns how to use money on his or her own and then we let the child chance into the future whilst aiming at all directions. The child will end up achieving nothing or will be trapped in a dangerous cage or end up wasting time. Just like sex, if you do not teach your child about it they will learn about it from others and may become vulnerable to negative influences.

The Montessori Model of Education is a popular model that can be used to train young children. The model advocates for children to explore and learn things on their own. It advises child care givers to enrich the child's environment with resources and let the child manipulate the resources in any way they can possibly imagine. In an environment with toys, the child may use one item for as many ways as possible, some constructive and others destructive. Give them a cup, they drink from it and urinate in it, then use the urine to make mad or use it to cook *ugali* with soil being the flour. The children may later break the cup to create a plate for *ugali* and *mboga*.

When children use this mode of education, they realize what is dangerous and what is palatable. This reminds me of the class two tales headlined "The grass soup." Two children decided to mimic their mum's way of cooking. They lit a fire, erected three stone support for the *sufuria*, picked an iron tin probably a paint or *kimbo* tin, put water in it and then added grass. Once the 'soup' had boiled they drunk it and were rewarded with stomach aches. When they could not stand the pain anymore, they quickly turned to their parents for help.

In many ways, this is one of the ways that we were introduced to the subject of money. As children grow, they gravitate towards the more comfortable and less energy sapping ways. They quickly learn how to spend and ask for more without stopping to think about the source of money. Children assume that their guardians do not love them when they are not given money and some may go as far as suing their parents for 'neglect.' However, by obliging and giving in into our children's whims, we miss an opportunity to teach them a vital lesson on money.

Pocket Money

A lesson camouflaged in emotions sticks more in our memories, whether painful or laughable. We all tend to clearly remember things in our childhood which embarrassed us. Try to instill a lesson to your children every time you give them money. Let them know the good side and the negative effects of money.

We grew up being given pocket money by our friends, parents, siblings and relatives but we were not told what it was for. You would be given school fees and told "This is school fees for the year or term." But when given pocket money, you are not told what it is for so we end up misusing the money. Whether the student spends the money or not is not anyone's problem since no one ever demands accountability for the pocket money. It is up to the student to determine where the money goes. No one really cares what they spend the money on be it is something illegal or not.

This reminds me of my secondary life. One day my friend was sent by our geography teacher to buy him a chapatti worth 10 shillings from the school canteen. He was given 100/= shillings note and he asked the teacher if he could keep change but the teacher refused. Keeping the change would have meant that he pockets 90 shillings. This is a common scenario in most of our homes. We send our children to buy things from the shops but rarely do we hold them accountable for any extra money that might have remained after purchasing the items.

Keeping change or not demanding it from the person using it is an artificial creation of a manipulation loophole. When the child's demands are met at home or school and they find themselves with more disposable income, then they have automatically found a way of making more money. When students have more money than they need, they start buying items that they do not really need, e.g. play stations, Ipads and designer clothes. They may start going for discos at a young age and avoid eating food offered by the school. In a worst case scenario, the students may start buying drug and booze.

During my school days, there were some students who never set foot in the kitchen precincts. If they ever went there they would be going for hot water or soup. The students would eat canteen food for a whole term and would be visited every month. Their boxes were always full of edibles, meaning the parents were oblivious of the use of school fees they paid. These students always complained of weevil ridden food and bad meals.

Some students go to the extent of devising creative ways which they employ to trick their parents into giving them more money. When I was in form two, I had a friend who came from a relatively rich family. His father owned many lorries, tractors and a number of transport vehicles. My friend, Charles, was always given a lot of money by his father but it was never enough. His pocket money was always insufficient for his prodigal lifestyle. He wore bling-bling accessories and relied on canteen food. Charles sneaked in and out of school and begun smoking at will. He would borrow money from other students whenever he ran out of money and end up in so many debts. In fact Charles used to borrow money than I did. It was unusual when he asked me to lend him money and yet the first money I ever received from my father was
150/=.

To me this was like banking a million shillings! I almost gave the money back to him or added to my fees because I always had a deficit. I asked him what the money was for since I did not understand why I needed the money while in school. Charles never paid the entire school fees that he was given; he would pay half and pocket the other amount. When other students were being sent away for books they had lost, he colluded with the prefects to obtain a school leave out to collect money for about five books. His father being a busy man never questioned him but innocently gave him the exact amount for the books.

Two months into every term when things were tight for him, Charles would sell his expensive items cheaply. Ironically ten years down the line, I bought the belt I wear today from him for only 100 shillings yet he had bought it at 300 shillings. Charles had a mentality that his father was rich and whatever his father had was his. This notion always put him high above the other students and some struggling teachers. Most of the time, he would be caught breaking school regulations and be punished. This never bothered him since punishments had become a common occurrence in his life.

Charles started smoking, drinking alcohol and sneaking out of school for discos all the time since he had money at his disposal. Charles came to school with expensive perfumes, deodorants and some skin lightening jellies that no one else in school could afford. Charles was dark but the chemical infested jellies made him too light skinned. These changes in his face left some dark spots and other brown cake like patches. The changes in his body tampered with Charles' self esteem. His fellow students disliked his body image so he isolated himself from others. He ended up feigning illness most of the time and slept while others were in class. This affected his end term results negatively. Charles bought more expensive jellies to counter the effects of the first ones from the pocket money that his father sent him. At times he duped his father into giving him more money.

On the first days of form three, Charles' father met the school deputy who on chatting learned that Charles had been given the school fees for the whole term. As a routine, anyone who had school arrears was sent home on the last Friday of the opening month. The deputy teacher was surprised when upon learning that Charles had arrears since he should have paid the money. Charles got into problems which earned him a suspension and later an expulsion from school.

Sometimes we deceive ourselves that giving students money is helping them. We give because we think that they expect it and the students end up believing that it is their right to be given money. But, do we as parents ever question the "pocket money" that we give? Why do we assume in case of emergencies the student would sort themselves with the money?

While in form one and two, Charles was among the students who stayed an extra day in school waiting for the accounts clerk to lend them some money to leave for home. Only an irresponsible student can consume everything they have by end term. Experience shows us that it is hard to stop a car on high speed downhill. Once they have been accustomed to a high living standard, even if they have a budget for transport and the one for high life is over shifting the vote is not an issue for them since refilling is always possible.

An issue which we usually do not communicate to our children is that we parents have what we have because we worked for it. What we have as parents only supports our children for some time and is not theirs for a lifetime. It is there to support their meals, clothing, housing, security, entertainment and education up to a certain time. When children know this, they are able to look up to their parents in order to learn and not receive money. Relative to young people should seek to learn a lot about money and life and transfer this knowledge to the children. They say that when you teach, you learn twice.

In most cases when you talk about something you have read or learnt, it forces you to think, become more creative, get mind boggling questions which challenge your beliefs as a whole.
Talking about money to our children can help us become better with money. In answering their funny innocent questions you think and widen your scope. Some of the questions I have met include:-

- Why go to school?
- Do you believe in the 8-4-4 system? Does it help anyone get money?
- If I did what I learnt today, will I get money?
- Does selling involve going to school?
- Have all rich people completed school?
- If you say one + one, what is this "one" and "one?"
- What is money?
- Where did money come from?
- Isn't money not for spending?
- Is money not for buying and paying for what we need?

Let's talk to our children about money. If we do not, they will listen to any hawker who most likely will manipulate them. A story is told of a man who for so long wanted to be rich. He sought advice from church leaders on how best this could be achieved, consulted friends, enemies, the rich and everyone he could think of. As his last resort, he went to the witchdoctors. As optimistic as he always was, he believed that everything is possible. After the goads had been kicked came the words that, "Whatever he touched would turn into money." This was to take effect the following morning. He was so thrilled that he could not wait for what would follow soon.

On waking up the following morning, the man touched his wife who immediately changed to money. He moved to the kitchen which turned into money, the plates, the *sufurias*, the chairs and everything he touched turned into money. This made him seethe. He decided to take breakfast from the nearby town hotels. On his way the friends he greeted turned into money. On arriving at the hotel he decided not to touch anything. As he was there he forgot and touched the table and chairs which became money. He became more angry and violent; breathing fire he converted the whole town into money.

This way he set on the path way frustrated, hungry and angry, despondent and introverted. He later decided to go back to the witchdoctor who had made him a money wizard to have the powers revoked. On arriving at the watchmen's place, he shook his hand amidst confusion that turned him into a pile of coins. There he was with lots of money but no food, no water, no trees for shade, no air, no friends nothing but money, listless he died a long slow death.

When giving financial advice to our young ones, let us also tell them that money is not everything but it is paramount in anything. People, hills, soil, sky, trees and books are important too. Let them not disregard all these in their quest to stuck notes in their pockets.

Pocket Money

Great lessons are drawn from little things in life. It is the simple things we do that counts. Jesus, the great teacher of the Bible used the parable of the mustard seed symbolizing the word of God. The parable talks about humble, minute beginnings to great heights. In the same way there are the simple things we say in our homes. They are the small whispers about money we utter that train our children more. They are the valueless 50 coins and ten cents coins buried in the soil or lost in a carton that could hold the greatest lessons about money to our children.

For instance, a small child who finds a 50 cent coin rushes to the mother to ask what it is. The mother tells the child it is dirty old money that needs to be discarded. To the mother, the coin has lost its value and deserves to be in the dust bin. The Government might have withdrawn the others and it may not have any value but to me it holds great life lessons.

LESSON 1: WORK
For that now useless coin to be somewhere someone must have earned it as it was not just given. Somebody had to work hard to get it. The worker who earned it either worked hard or smartly to pocket it. By working, I mean trading of individual skills, time and energy against a salary or a wage.

LESSON 2: TAXES
That there is an institution by the name government, which reduces the amount of salaries and wages one should get. The 50 cents or 10 cents in the household should be part of the remainder after the Government takes some part away.
The Government agreed to be taking part of the salaries of workers and consumers and in return provide security and infrastructure or what individuals cannot provide for themselves.

LESSON 3: MONEY IS ALWAYS ON TRANSIT

Money in whatever form is helpful when used. Its use requires change of ownership. Money is not useful since you cannot cook and eat it, you cannot travel in it, you cannot cloth it but you can only use what it is worth in terms of food, clothes, fare etc and this way the coins, cash, cheques, Mpesa,

Zap, Yu cash money, Iko pesa are always on transit. Therefore retaining that coin there denied it a chance to circulate further at its life time.

LESSON 4: MONEY LOSSES VALUE

These 50 cents coins or the holed coins have no value because they are worth nothing which can be sold. You carry it to the market and the traders won't accept it. This means that the coins that have value are of greater numbers like one shilling and more. Although two 50 cents coins have a value of one shilling, the one shilling coin can buy something but the 50 cents cannot buy anything. That money of the lowest denomination loses its ability to stand for goods and services with time. Even in years to come, that one shilling coin will eventually lose its value.

LESSON 5: GROWING THE 50 CENTS

Money increases by multiplying it. The 50 cents can grow to one shilling, from one shilling to 25 shillings, and then more. Considering the 50 cents can buy a sweet, then one can buy one sweet and instead of eating it you hulk the sweet into two pieces and sell each piece 50 cents which are equivalent to one shilling. Using the one shilling you can look for somewhere where oranges cost one shilling. You buy it then divide it into four pieces then sale each piece for 50 cents equivalent to 2 shillings. It grows when in use and loses value when just kept.

LESSON 6: METAL VALUE OF THE COIN

The coin itself may be worth nothing present today in the market, but that doesn't mean it's place is in the dust bin. The coin is made of some valuable metal, be it copper or silver. These coins can be sold as scrap metal. This way the coins are worth but cannot buy things in the market. The metal used to make the coin can be mounded into something different.

Seizing the Moment

There is no particular time and place where learning by our children cannot take place. In its natural sense, learning cannot fail to happen because it is inevitable and continuous. When you are not teaching your child, they are learning. Many are times we ask ourselves questions like when do I start teaching my child about money? According to me, the question is not when you will start teaching your child about money; it is how much has the child learnt from me so far.

We need to behave in ways that our children can emulate positively. The child may be young, may not say much and may be inactive but the way they are, but they know that they can emulate you as their parent. Earn in ways they can earn, spend in ways they can spend, save in ways they can save, grow your money in ways they can grow, invest in ways they can invest and keep your money in ways they can keep.

The young in terms of money are perfect believers in the Japanese philosophy; tell them and they will forget, show them and they will remember but engage them and they will understand. When all you do is talk about money, then the chances of them forgetting everything you have said are higher. By showing someone is when you show them a price list, a budget for their school, show them a saving box and

37

they will not buy your idea. Involving them when drawing a family budget so that they can know what items are to be prioritized and learn how to make shopping lists. They also know how you compare prices from Nakumatt, Tuskys and Uchumi and wholesale outlets. This way they learn money tricks faster.

Engaging them fully involves them joining you on the real buying of these items so that they can see you do the actual purchase. They can see you bargain, ask for discounts, and ask for transport by the staff so they learn how to negotiate.
My sister was surprised when she learnt that one can ask for discounts in a chemist. My elder brother had sent her and mother to the hospital for check up. At the hospital they were advised by the doctor to purchase some medications from the chemists in town.

They paid one thousand two hundred shillings at the pharmacist for the medicine. My brother asked how much discount they had been given after looking at the receipts.
When the dose was over, the brother went to the same chemist and he was given a discount of 200/= hence ended up paying 1000/=.

One big lesson in purchasing is that goods are always produced with the end consumer in mind. Be it sweets, TVs, chocolates, drugs, vehicles etc. Many people are involved in the distribution channel and every one of them tries to keep their profit higher. On the other hand consumers have in mind, having the most of a product or service for the least price. The buyer and seller are protagonists, each pulls their way. When our young children hear us challenge the sellers they realize the prices they have set are not law and learn by modeling and physically being involved.

Pocket Money

What makes the buyer passionate about keeping the price low is the cost they had to pay to earn their money. Before they had it to spend they had to earn it. They earned it by using their time, energy and skill to a willing buyer. When it comes to students who haven't spent time, energy or have acquired any skill but are given money, the propensity to spend and even pay more for things they would have paid less increases.

It is not because they have mostly earned it. It is because we learned to give because we were given or not given or even because we have it. The biggest challenge is training young people on how to spend money they have not earned. How one learns to spend their pocket money affects their spending habits when they get employed and start earning. For instance, my friend Susan learnt from their short high school trips to buy things from supermarkets during their short outings from school to symposiums, games and debates sessions outside the school. They would be given five minutes by their teachers to get into a supermarket and buy whatever they wanted and get back into their school bus.

Since time was short, she would pick things in hurry without much keenness on its use or way of consuming it. Ten years later she works in Nairobi City. Due to pressure of work she passes in some areas sees something good buys it and her first question is how it is eaten or used. She could not use some of the things she bought so she ended up throwing them away. This is a wasteful habit that she learned when she had money that she used yet had not earned. The habit continues when she is now earning.

Anything in the realm of the child or young person's reality can be used to enhance their relationship with money. Ask them whether they know the price of the book they are asking for, the price of the pencil, the price of cars, types of cars and their costs. Ask them why everyone around them doesn't have what they have? Or have what they do not have? Always capture the moment and pass information.

When teaching children about money, live the life you want them to. Talk about things or experiences the way you want them to talk. If you are abusive about money they will abuse it more than you. Every generation tries to advance more than the previous one. Watch what you do with money in their presence for they may double or triple your tribulations with money.

Harv E. in his book, "Secrets of Millionaires Mind" recognizes three ways in which our thinking about money is embedded. He notes that verbal programming especially for young children informs their thinking about money. Verbal programming are words from authority figures which stick in a child's mind and influence their thinking even at old age.
In the age old debate of whether a child's brain is a Tabula Vasa or contains information.

Assuming we choose John Locke's explanation that a child's brain is born without anything but an empty slate ready for knowledge. Every word you say, anything the child observes is a candidate for imprinting in their slate. Since birth the mind opens files for different information i.e. a money file, relationship file, food files, etc. Every word, event or experience that happens the child's mind sorts it and records it appropriately for later use. This later use informs our thinking.

Pocket Money

The words a mother says, a father, school teacher, uncles, aunts, police, counselors etc have a heavy toll on a young person's mind and life. As you grew up you might have heard words like, we do not grow money, your father has not been paid, work hard and you will have a lot of money, the rich also cry, the rich are corrupt, for you to be rich you must know somebody, hard work pays and much more. Looking back, these words about money have channeled me into the rat race. Chasing something and being obsessed with it but nothing to show at the end of it all. Chasing a pay that ends at the start of every month. This area of money is only just one.

A perfect example of verbal programming is words I heard a mother tell her daughter and later saw her live the words. In the year 2003, I heard a mother of five tell her last born nasty words. The mother in question, *Jane dropped out of school in standard five. She got children early from her marriage which lasted for some time. Her words were sharp to anyone including her children. Since her last born never left the radius of her dress she got programmed by her mother.

One particular incident, I overheard as I got close to them on the way were the words *"Uilye ata we kowisa kusyaiya kwenyu,"* (You look like you will have children before you get married). These are the words I heard in 2003. In the year 2010, to my surprise, I saw Jane in the company of policemen heading to her neighbors homestead. The police wanted to find out why Jane followed her daughter everywhere she went. In response, Jane explained that her daughter was naughty, abusive and was attending discos every night. She had left school at standard two and was arrested during her examinations as she was already expectant.

41

The point is, parents should monitor what they say to their children. Parents, relatives and teachers have authority and their words are very powerful. You call a child stupid and they live up to that, you call them clever and they live up to it. You utter the words "you spend thrift" and they really become spendthrifts. You utter the words "money manager" and your child becomes a money manager, you say the words you "wicked child" and they truly become wicked in their ways.

Our words are so powerful such that one may believe that many people today are failures in their lives simply because their mothers called them stupid, their teacher called them you fool, their friend laughed at them, their pastor said they could not make it or their fathers said they could not make it. Others are successful because words of faith and self belief were breathed in them all through. These words have the effect of denting the child's self concept hence lowering their self esteem.

Some parents and guardians have no faith in their sons or daughters that they would rather risk work to walk to school or drive to school to pay school fees. Walking to school with your child, carrying their school fees assumes they cannot understand and cannot handle money. They may lose it, misuse it or miraculously find they do not have it. This communicates something to the particular child. The child learns that they are considered irresponsible with money and cannot be trusted with risky issues. When doing that to a child, what do you expect of such a teenager when they graduate from college never having carried their college fee?
What about when they get their first pay cheque?

Won't they experience some sweet freedom and end up purchasing with all their income? Won't they become stingy with money? Won't they not develop a negative attitude towards money and hence usher in lack of money instead of luck? What is the effect on your child of whatever exposure you are providing especially in relation to money? Do you ever seek feedback of what they think of what you do to them?

In my practice, I liked an experience of one particular student who is a mother. After learning such concepts of family communication loops and system interactions, she went home and after supper deliberately sought feedback. She came up with certain questions which allowed her husband and children to verbalize their experiences. Some of the questions included: -

- What makes you proud of being a member of this family?
- What areas are going on well?
- What are the areas that need improvement?
- What do you think of school going children?
- What areas of your schooling do you like?
- What areas would you wish changed and how?
- How can we as a family work on whatever areas we have identified as needing improvement?

This particular mother was overjoyed with the effect of this particular discussion in their family. She says that in the morning after everyone would wake up with renewed vigor and a sense of direction. The boys and girls swept the compound like they wanted it clean. The morning tea was sweeter with the ingredients perfectly mixed. The children left for school owning the whole course. The kiss from the husband was even more assuring that night and morning before he left for work. Everybody seemed to have had the right dose, the right amount at the right moment. Even the cats, dogs, calves, kids and lambs seemed to sense the change in the atmosphere. The environment breathed confidence.

According to her, she had made a practice and it freed all in the family to share their challenges, seek help and offer help whenever the need arose. It worked for her and her family. Even in areas where money was a problem, the children being sent home from school and staying at home helped energize them instead of belittling them. The reason being they understood sometimes the farm paid their fees and being at home was a chance for them to educate themselves.

Open round of sharing worked for her. I do not know what would work in your situation, being the one who knows your family situations; past and where you want to go. Be creative and you will avert unforeseen situations and trouble.

An article on the Saturday Women Instinct Magazine of October 2, 2010, "Tame that mischievous tongue" reads, *"Why do you always seat at the corner alone like a thief?"* That is the question Mary Wanjiku was always asked by her mother when she was still a young girl. Mary was the quiet type and would sit silently at a corner and watch sheepishly as the rest of the family enjoyed a chat. And true to her mother's confession, Mary turned out to be a wanted criminal and got married to a most wanted gangster- Bernard Matheri alias "Rasta". Mary started stealing at the age of 14; she stole Ksh.70, 000.00 from her grandmother who used to keep the tithe for her church. Luckily for Mary, she got born again and is now a preacher.
Moral of the story is that you should watch what comes out of your mouth. The tongue is a little organ that can cause so

much harm to people. Those little nothings you keep saying to either your child or yourself will one day manifest into reality.

Reading this article brings to mind two things; verbal programming and the law of attraction. Mary Wanjiku's mother verbally programmed her daughter to become a thief. She heard the word 'thief' many times that she lived to be one. She started early and young and they say charity begins at home. She started at home by stealing her grandmother's kitty. Then she perfected the skill with age.

On the flip side, her focus on transferring and owning other peoples things without their consent attracted those of the same kind. The person attracted was a larger and more active in stealing. The lesson is that what we focus on expands and attracts more of similar kind. Watch what you tell your child and what you say to yourself.

CHAPTER 3

THE MISSING
LINKS

Pocket Money

 T he Oxford Dictionary defines a link as a person or thing that
connects two other people or things. Our education systems fail to
connect class subjects and money. If they bond, it is either by
selling real products or being employed to earn salaries. These are
the only revealed secrets. Many links that are keys to success are
left implicit. These links are left to be gleaned from the
environment, from old sayings that hold
and keep the un-eyed on tasks forever.

Grades And Living Standards

In one of my counseling classes, I was handling the topic on
what causes change. My focus was on the different models
of dealing with people's issues. What really causes change?
We can get the answer to this based on the theoretical
perspective. If it is a behavioral problem, then probably it is
a learned behavior and change would occur through un-
learning the behavior. If it is cognitive, then change of
thought would lead to alteration of behaviour and the other
theoretical perspectives.

The discussion veered off when a student gave an eye opening
story. Salma Ali, the student, is a high school teacher in North
Eastern Kenya. High school students who perform well in this
region qualify to attend teacher's colleges, universities, medical
colleges and other middle level colleges. These students
become the village creams and hopefuls for the entire village.
The students are trained through government assistance like
Joint Admission Board (JAB), Constituency Development Fund
(CDF), Local Authority Transfer Fund (LATF) and other
agencies and are later employed in the local schools,
dispensaries and agricultural offices as civil servants.
This enables them to retain their respect as enviable society
members.

However, with the meager taxed government salaries they fail to make it big in life and only succeed in becoming slaves to their salaries. They fail to budget or save for the little that they get at the end of the month. Salma Ali explained that an inverse relation existed in her region and she fell in this category. Salma was trying to get out of the cycle but somehow still maintained it. She hoped that the Teachers' Service Commission (TSC) would grant her a salary increment after her counseling diploma. This was her way of getting out of the system.

Most of the rich people in her province are school dropouts. After one or two years of leaving school they get some bearing and are mentored in starting up some form of business. Therefore the well educated work for the less educated. People who work as teachers, nurses and government administrators willingly pay school dropouts. This is the case because the dropouts own the transport means, *dukas,* petrol stations, milling industries, rental premises and anything else these people ever needed. If you look at education from this perspective then school grades fail to directly lead to high living standards. The other class participants confirmed similar cases in different parts of the country.

I am by no means against people who support noble tasks in the society since they play a vital role in our growth. My point is that salaries alone rarely lead to high living standards. Money experts propose that paid earning needs to be turned into a passive type of income, that is, income earned by doing nothing.

Michael Joseph, a former Kenya's and East and Central Africa's most accomplished company CEO said, "To make it in life, you need to achieve something more than a degree," (The Standard Newspaper Wednesday 29/09/2010). This was during an educational talk to students of Visa Oshwal Academy Senior high. His words indirectly told all who were present that you need much more than schooling to live your life's ambitions.

In the same way, grades alone are not a guarantee or a determinant to better living standards, satisfactory income, a good car, a good house or security. It takes something more than a good grade to achieve all these. A teacher from Makueni Secondary School, one of the top performing secondary schools, made me realize that many brilliant students end up frustrated despite possessing enviable certificates. They are paid poor or subjected to harsh working conditions. The teacher, Mrs. Muli, shared how the stringent schedule of events at their school had turned the teachers and students into result-producing machines. The school's routine had conditioned students to lose sleep by 3.00am but this did not hinder the students from dozing in class from 11pm.

A student proceeded home after KCSE after going through the normal school routines and attained an A. With the system still in his blood, he would lose sleep most of the hours. Without much of a delay, he joined University to pursue a degree in medicine. Medicine wasn't enough for him therefore he added CPA and emerged top in the country. On finishing his degree program, he got a job in Wajir as a government medical doctor. With his programmed mind, he drowned himself in work but failed to derive much satisfaction from it.

Maria Montessori, the Italian doctor believed that education is a natural process spontaneously carried out by the human individual, and is acquired not by listening to words, but by experiences upon the environment. The teacher's role is to prepare a series of motives of cultural activity spread over a specially prepared environment, and refrain from obtrusive interference. For those who believe the individuals mind is an empty slate, Montessori challenges them with the above example.

What the man in the above allusion tries to do is to endure with what was placed before him, priced in the environment, esteemed, and coveted by many as they perspire in their aspirations. This is not what he naturally gravitated towards, but what the chances around him narrowed to channel his efforts, time and energy. He may now have to endure boring sessions with patients, long working hours dealing with lives negatives and peoples pains could be in the Montessori's model. This particular doctor could have ended in a different career i.e. music, business or journalism which could flow with much ease.

Maria Montessori wrote, "And if education is always to be conceived along the same antiquated lines of a mere transmission of knowledge, there is little to hope for it in the bettering of mans future, for what is the use of transmitting knowledge if the individual's total development lags behind?" This helps us understand the need amongst many people who have been funneled into careers by the system spreading the desire tentacles into careers after they are first employed.
Changing careers is not a problem even at sixty years you have advanced your education level.

1. 1+1, 2+2, 1+3
In our initial orientation in education we are initiated into the numerical values and letters. We were taught that there are integers 0-9. These were mathematically introduced as numbers. We learnt they existed, we sung them in songs and dance and they stuck in us for good. Our continuous use of these numbers made the difference in life.

Pocket Money

The point is – many systems of education in the world introduce learners to inanimate items, blocks, tools in a similar way. In my early learning in nursery school and standard one, we were required always to have 100 sticks in our bags as learning aids. The interesting thing is that just as we were taught, we still teach our children today to think the same way. We tell them that integers represent things in the environment which need to be counted, such as trees, objects and cows.

What we were not told is that the one + one really should refer to us as humans. In this particular wisdom left for our deduction, lays the big secret that has been utilized by successful people over the years. One + one mean, my mind + another mind, hence a larger one that is more adaptable to the environment. It means my talent added to another talent creates a more eased survivor. The larger one, generally referred to as two, is a combination of the previous single talents, voices, minds, forces, energies. The two when added to other twos or ones elsewhere enlarges the single unit being created. The unit therefore encompasses many talents working as one, voices speaking as one or minds working as one etc.

This is something that no one really tells us. The colonialists secretively put it in our minds that counting people is an invitation for a bad omen. In reality, the colonialist was trying to put asunder what people generally knew and practiced. This strategy worked and continues to plaque us all. People usually think and do things like during the colonization era.

The greatest link is not just one cow added to another, then to goats, then sheep and horses to form a herd. The greatest and missing link is when people think and act uniquely. It is about heightening the individualistic attitude ingrained and watered by the divide and rule principles. School going children are left to implicitly glean from the wisdom of counting trees, sticks, stones and strokes in books.

Nature laws have endowed us with complimentary and supplementary energies, forces, talents and gifts. If we put our talents together then we can produce more than we can imagine. The gift of a rancher and veterinary doctor combined makes them both rich; the gift of voice and a microphone maker pulls a larger crowd. The wisdom is that, an individual's talent even if it is the same as that of the other persons, when combined can earn much more with much ease.

Companies merge so that they can supplement or complement each other. One company may be good at production and weak at distribution but when they combine their operations with another company they earn more. This should apply to individuals too, not just to man made things. Human beings can apply this principle on other things that they do not glean and tap this great wisdom.

In the law of attraction there are two dimensions brought forth; like attracts like. Birds of the same feather flock together the same as opposites attract. These two propositions are highly debatable, but they hold water in the way natural endowments in people are distributed. Two bright students who are close can go further in life. Two shrewd investors can sharpen each other. Two companies dealing with similar products can combine forces, e.g. Orange and Kenya Telecom made Kenya Telecom reach wide communities and offer wireless phones with much ease while Orange also chanced into Kenya.

Pocket Money

On the contrary proposition that opposites attract. It is also naturally put that the short and tall can achieve more together than either alone. A mathematician and a linguist can help one another to achieve more. When a production company combines forces with distributors, then the profits increase.
At a class level, students can easily combine their forces to accommodate each other's strengths and weaknesses in subjects.

Just as iron sharpens iron, man has the ability to sharpen the other. This is proving that one + one, two + two brings out a more wise, stronger two. The same principle is used by politicians in coalition building. They exploit unity in diversity by uniting their clans to be a community, merging communities and using the term 'we.' This is what has guided and built many politicians for the longest time possible. Company owners tend to focus on who works best with others when hiring their staff.

To succeed everyone must carry out a self analysis, fight the spirit of individualism and seek to merge efforts with like-minded or complimenting individuals. This brings better results. It is so funny how people can sit together in the same place, neighborhood or in a *matatu* but fail to say hi to each other. We decide to ignore the people around us yet; we can sell each other's products, know the source of raw materials needed by another person and know the perfect market for each other's produce. The natural law of attraction is at work so you easily attract what you focus on.

Technology encourages individualism. One gets in a public vehicle sits to a potential customer, distributor, partner, security and wears earphones enjoying their music in solitude. This doesn't help; say hi? And the results will be marvelous.

There are things in this world that have been equally given to us by our creator. The difference comes in how we utilize the resources that are around us. Some people may fail to know that these resources exist while others do not know whether they really are resources. Some may realize that they have resources at their disposal but still fail to utilize them. People who succeed in life fully realize the nature and value of these resources and go full throttle in making use of them. Others on realizing how these resources are try to lull the masses who in essence are part of the resources.

If you attended an interview and you are asked what one plus one (1+1) is what would you answer? Is the answer two, three, a big one. To me the best answer would be "what one wants it to be!"

2. 24 HOURS FOR ALL

If the assertion that 24 hours makes a day is true, then we all have 24 hours in a day. A day by an operational definition means a day (with natural light) approximately 12 hours and a night of approximately 12 hours totaling to 24 hours. The number of days which these precious time is available matters as days turn into weeks, months, years, decades and centuries. A look at time in decades, year, month, day, hour after hour makes differences in persons. Two people who have lived in the same decade usually have different results to show purely based on how they used their time.

Within the vital 24 hours in a day some work more than others and so according to what they do; some earn more than others. Some sleep less and earn more while others who are sleepless earn less. Consider a maid who is employed to work in a household with major tasks as household chores.
She wakes up before everyone and sleeps after everyone has snored in the household. Some city hustlers wake up

very early to catch the earliest vehicles before the fares hike and head to their different workplaces. In the evening the same people have to wait for nightfall for the fares to soar downwards before they head home.

Consider this, in the same city, some people wake up as early as 3.00am to prepare for a long day, the norm rather than the exception. The alarm clock has become the hall mark of their success. Those who by 8.00am have worked for 5 hours through reading, planning and carrying out research and wait to feed the masses when they wake up. Others stretch their day to the middle of the night, thanks to lights and their control of the environment. Consider a track driver hauling goods from Mombasa to Congo Brazzaville with slight stop over at various centers. Compare what they earn verses their bosses. Their employers call it a day and wake up at 10.00am to ask if the goods have been delivered.

My colleagues and I were transferred to one of our office branches set up in the woods. We usually arrived at our hotel at around 11pm and the receptionist happily ushered us to a nearby table and invited the waiter. After stuffing our tummies we were led to our rooms and were surprised when the hotel owner said to us, "When you sleep this early when do you ever plan for your life? Will you ever become rich?" We feigned fatigue –which surely we were. His comments sounded like rebuke to a hard worker having toiled the whole day. His words rang in our heads as we got in our beds cold beds. According to him we had just arrived to plan for a big kill to come or how to move a mountain on our way, yet we were just commoners.

The secret lies in the fact that many of the people are endowed with the 24 hours but have no clue on how to utilize them. The rich know how to use their time while the poor have their time spend by the rich. The rich employers mainly utilize their 24 hours and offer to pay those who do not know what to do with their time. This statement might sound indicative to noble servants and satisfied workers. However, time will always remain the ultimate determinant. Employers are fully aware that their workers have time but do not know how to use it. That is why they keep workers around them with overtime; paid leave days etc. How do you use your ultimate resource time? Is it being utilized by another?

My boss once told us a story of how he sealed loopholes in time wasted by construction workers. He realized that they spend time smoking, so he made a law against smoking. The workers spent more time during tea and lunch break so he let them be served with the tea and lunch at the work place. He realized that the workers hobbled on their way to the lavatories so he timed them and whoever spend more than a minute was fined 200/=. The workers at times arrived to work late and left early, so he made a law against lateness and leaving early. He also opted to put a watchman at the gate so that workers who spent most of their time with their visitors could be penalized. In no time, the rate of tank construction increased from one to three tanks per week.

People who know the secrets to success do not hawk their time around. They do not usually write resumes detailing how much time they have to give away and at what cost. The rich know that the many poor people have a lot of time to hawk, that is why most people are given meager salaries for the time they spend since if one is not willing to trade at that price, someone else will. Look at many industries in Athi River, Industrial Area Nairobi and flower farms in Naivasha in the morning, you find many people flooded at the gates ready to bargain for the time they have that day. If one fails to secure a chance then they count the day wasted since no one is willing to pay or purchase those hours.

Many people do not know that the biggest secret to being wealthy lies in changing ones position. Instead of grappling all day, seize any opportunity in front of you and start using others' disposable time. This means you start a business or project and utilize others time. This way, you occupy your time and work faster. Many people have used the concept of paying others for the man hours that they have invested in working for them and are reaping the fruits.

Man hours and people willing to offer the time might attract different prices in the market based on the experience, level of education and dexterity of skill. Whether we are employed to work in an office, farm, roads and oceans, part of what we put on the table are the hours. Time is given to us equally but we attract wealth in different quantities during these 24 hours.

- How much are you earning in 24 hours now?
- Are there others earning higher than you within the same time? Definitely yes?
- What are they doing that you are not doing?
- What can you do to increase your output in 24 hours?
- If within an education system, are you doing more than the rest in 24 hours?

Look around you and learn the way being applied by those earning more than you. They may be sleeping and relaxing more, yet earning more or vice versa.

3. THE INTEGERS 0-9 AND LETTERS A-Z

Since the invention of writing styles and the numerical numbers, these numbers are available to everyone. They range from 0-9 no more or less. These are not just numbers but are resources. Looking at numbers as resources makes a big difference. How we use these numbers makes a difference between one person and another. You can combine these numbers in any way and achieve whatever is in one's imagination.

We use numbers to represent or quantify our possessions and our wealth and that's that. Using numbers for quantification was used during the pre-colonial period before the colonialists introduced their system of counting and quantifying possessions. A case in point is indicated during dowry negotiations and payment of the same, each side involved used to document what they received or took to the other family.

In the Kamba tradition, each family involved in dowry negotiations kept a string with which they recorded what they received. If a man was to take 46 goats, then each time he took a goat to his wife's parents he would tie a knot on his string and the girl's parents would do the same. This practice went on till all the goats were paid. This is counting using integers.

How we use numbers and the meaning we attach to them makes a huge difference. People have used these ten numbers, 0-9, as resources and not just as counting symbols. Many writers have written books and sold many copies mainly using numbers. Combining these numbers in conjunction with letters makes an individual rich.

Still either in the Cuneiform or Hieroglyphics forms of early writing by the Sumerians and Egyptians, the invention of letters which form the languages we speak today is also a resource. Many people have used the letters a-z and have grown rich. Master piece creations using these a-z letters have been spoken, written, and made many people rich. Books have been written; speeches have been given and have made many people rich. People looked at the letters a-z and numbers 0-9 as resources and as tools and became millionaires.

As part of the early learning education systems in the world, these letters and numbers are introduced to learners. Children are mainly taught to use numbers and letters for communication. Mainly letters are pieced together in certain ways to convey a certain message and to tell a story. Since the main aim is to communicate, then those who see these as resources take it two vital elements of communication further and choose to deliver their message to wider crowds and make more money.

Like the experts' advice raise your energy and when people crowd near you, bill them. Writers, speakers, media stations print and telecommunication rely on the letters A-Z, 0-9 or those available in the other languages. They coin messages with the same letters and make money. The masses use what the media has to make money from them, few realize this.
Largely, education systems depend on these letters and integers to encode their message. Education institutions rely on these letters and numbers to decode their message and pass the same to the masses hence making millions.

Change your view of the numbers 0-9 and letters A-Z. Look at them as resources and not just as merely communication symbols. Write letters and books, carry out researches, novels, poems, lyrics, songs, give speeches and write songs even if you cannot sing them, someone else will. Open your eyes and see the newspaper you read daily, the internet you surf daily, book stores and libraries exist because of the 10 numbers and

26 letters in the English language or other language symbols and letters.

See this as an opportunity and change your perception. Do not just grapple, tell people your story, believe in the story and your passion will attract your market.

4. COLOR

Color is the hue that gives matter some flavor to the sight.
There are very many colors that are at the disposal of billions of people. Color doesn't exist to those with no eyes. Color when looked as an opportunity makes a lot of difference. This is almost a universal endowment to mankind but its usage differs. Color has made people earn their living and even enriched them.

Consider the early school days when art and craft was a compulsory subject. We learnt how to generate any color from the primary colors red, yellow and blue. Then, we could squeeze green color from tomato leaves and other available plants. The problem was that what we learnt was left at the school gates the moment we stepped out. Our greatest mistake was discarding the information that we were given once the art teacher left the classroom. Those who took it further are making money from it.

Consider Marangi, a paint advertiser with Dura Coat. Paint companies exist because they rely on colors to tinge their paint. Nutritionists flavor their delicacies with colors; road constructors paint the roads black with yellow and white stripes. The clothes we wear are dyed with color, and shoes are hued whilst houses, books, and paintings have color.
Everything around us is a combination of colors. Colors attract our attention so advertisements are spiced with colors.
Color is a cheap natural resource available to many of us. How

many are using it? Are you earning from using color? What can you do with color that can get you an extra coin? Must you be talented to use color to earn? You will be surprised that you get nothing from it. You may use the talented and earn credit.

Look at color as a resource given to us by the creator of the universe. He is a creator and He created us in His image. Therefore you are also a creator. The use of colors is widespread. Look around and you will notice that everything has some element of color in it. Somebody or something appears more attractive or dull based on the colors that we see. Events, professions, national and institution flags are represented by colors.

May the scales upon your eyes fall and enable you to engage in activities that earn more from this naturally available resource that others are using. Associate yourself with a person who knows how your talent can be traded. If you do not know what to do with your gift, learn. Do not be embarrassed that you do not know something instead seek to learn and enhance yourself.

5. THREADS

A thread is the fabric that knits our clothes, curtains and coverings. Since no one is devoid of accessing these strings, it can be counted as a valuable endowment to human kind. However, we know about it but fail to use it. Those who use thread have the ability to clothe us, cover our beds with bedding and decorate our houses with nice curtains. They have realized that no one will ever go naked hence thread products market is guaranteed. Even though women may tend to nudity, they will never deny a thread entrepreneur a chance to earn from them, besides their male counter parts tend to over dress hence compensate for lack of clothed femurs of our ladies.

During the 8-4-4 system when art and craft was a norm in primary schools, pupils learnt many uses of strings. We looked at different formations and how wafts and wefts formed large rolls of lined clothes. We learnt the different stitches at our disposal that help bring together lacerated clothe, shoe, facilities and even body parts by doctors and many other uses.

We once went to advertise a certain college in the Meru Agricultural Show. During the show, I walked around and visited all the stands available but forgot about all of them. However, one particular self-help group managed to bring memories of my art and craft lessons back to life. I had learnt about wafts and wefts fifteen years earlier and machines used to sew them together. I could never fathom what all this was then but the show opened up my thinking. I learnt how strings turn into cloth and acquired any design of any length and color.

I stood at this stand and looked at what I was wearing. I was astonished that simple machines that were manually operated wove such beautiful pieces. The turbines moved and the clothes made were the same as the clothes we wore. All types of clothes were on display. The particular self help group had many things on display. The string brought them together, fed them, clothed them and consumed their time but in the long run they earned from it. It made them travel and explore, it made them friends, it dissolved wrangles among them and enabled them to dine and wine rather than pine and age. The thread was a source of their many different conversations.

With nostalgia, I remember those days when my parents and older siblings had to make strings from sisal leaves. Each one of them had a number of the strings to work on daily. My parents always produced a larger pile of the sisal threads. My father had to prove a point by doing a larger pile of sisal threads than my mother's. The sisal threads then clothed us, fed us and educated us. It was the main source of income. We lived because of the sisal thread.

Many companies have been established in Kibwezi, some parts of Taita and other parts of Kenya because of sisal thread. They have employed and support many people in search of the thread. The employers in these sisal estates see the sisal thread as the real employer. The employees simply carefully cut the thorny ugly plants in haste. The thread has made companies; it has made colonialists stick around long after independence.

The message is that almost 100% of our bodies are always covered at 95% of the time, whether awake or asleep. The thread covers us young or old, lean or plump, shy or courageous, tall or short. We all need clothes. Count it joy if you now know that every person is a market for thread products from their toes to their head hair.

Many people who have been left to handle threads are those in polytechnics and considered low class or failures. This is a delusional way of looking at things. There is a lot one can do with the strings. The market is rich, wide and growing. Look at the thread which is an available a resource that has been used to earn money and not as something that doesn't exist.

The rich look at sisal as an opportunity to make many more billions. The have-nots look at it as work for the less civilized people. Being civilized is about wearing clothes and clothing others is making money; fashion is about money, mending lacerated clothes is making money. How are you using the thread? How else can you use it? How is your tailor using it?

Are you earning from threads? Remember you do not have to touch a thread to earn from it.

6. SOUND

Sound can be referred to as something that you hear or that can be heard. It is also said to be energy that travels in vibrations and is only received by the ears. Sound is top on the list of the things which were naturally provided to us. The creator of living things gave them the sense of hearing to hear energy movements strong enough to arouse curiosity to their ears. People who do not know what is causing the sound still use their ears. They know when they strike on something people will turn their attention to them.

The largest percentages of people have an active sense of hearing. Investors and shrewd entrepreneurs know this fact and capitalize on it. It is quite inevitable not to hear sounds in the surrounding. Because of the sense of hearing radio stations exist, T.V programs have sound, phones exist, speakers of all kinds have been invented to reach more hears and pass a message.

Sound has created a platform for advertisers, it has made an opportunity for teachers to go to class at any level, politicians win voters, preachers win souls, couples marry, rulers rule and reign on the masses and wars are fought. Everyone knows that people have ears and hear. Shrewd entrepreneur feed this yawning sense.

This is why whenever there are sudden sounds in an environment people rush to hear more. The sole reason why masses die in explosions is sound. Detractors understand this principle that is why they arrange several blasts, the first to attract people then the other to kill them.

Pocket Money

This is based on the natural law that the universe doesn't allow any vacuum to exist. If the ears cannot catch any sound then this law is not being obeyed. That is why whispers go far. People know secrets are shared in low tones hence they heighten their hearing sense to capture more.

Hawkers sing in praise of their items, *makangas* and *manambas* shout directions of their vehicles, con men and women build crowds by appealing to the ears. Musicians become house hold names because they produce sound which is music to the listener's ears, news presenters and news anchors survive by aiming for their audience's ears.

Most of us have a voice that can make any sound we wish. Whether the sound is organized or unorganized it is sound and has its place in the ears. How many ways can you use your voice? Just singing? Teaching? Preaching? Praying? Talking? Broadcasting? How many ways are possible for you? What do you have to do to use your voice in another way and earn from it? You could be a *makanga* so try and diversify your marketing skills to other areas. If you are a teacher try teaching in different places and teach different things to earn more. As a preacher, preach about the gospel of Christ but also be an advocate for the environment, not just heaven and yet our earthly problems remain unsolved.

Consider your voice as an asset that is to be treasured and used to produce more. Consider earning from the use of your voice in different ways. Do not be limited by your thinking.
People are not poor in possession, the poverty that wrecks and colonizes is that of thought, a thought stemming from a distorted reality past or self imprisonment.

7. PRESENCE OF OTHERS

Our creator ensured that we are born in a community; we grow within a community, wine and dine with a community, age within a community, mature, reproduce and die within a community. Living in the midst of people is a major resource and many people recognize this as an asset and a resource.

How an individual views themselves in the presence of others makes the difference. The perspective we have of those around us determines what we do in their presence. If other people use us, then we should use them, for instance a milk man sees neighbors who do not herd cows as a potential market. A *chang'aa* brewer sees everyone as a potential drunkard, a matatu tout sees everyone as a potential passenger and preachers see everyone around them as potential followers - sinners to be taken to heaven.

A story is told of a large crowd that attended the burial of a villager. People attend funerals to mourn specific losses.

Everyone present is usually guided by the loss they are experiencing. One of the politicians's who had attended the funeral said 'remorsefully' that he had lost the deceased's vote. The preacher mourned the loss of tithe, *zakat* and offering while the government representative grieved over the loss of a faithful tax payer. The shopkeeper knew he had lost a faithful customer and the partner grieved over the loss of a warm blanket when in need. The children mourned for they knew they now no longer had the love of a mother and father as the man's friend mourned an ardent drink buyer. My point is everyone around you looks at you from the point of their own benefit.

We live with others and cannot decide to live as islands. How we look at people around us determines our success in life. Some view others as stepping stones to greater heights, but not as a painful protruding that hurt the flesh. If you want to succeed in anything that you do then know who you are, who you are with and how to deal with everyone.

People who start companies, organizations and institutions know they need people to make it. For them to succeed they have to warm the best out of their employees. For instance, when they start a school they seek to make the teachers satisfy their curiosity of imparting knowledge, the security guards to feel their work is important, the cooks to better and put their recipes into use and the government officer to have work to inspect. In the end when the institution is running well, the teachers, cooks, guards and other workers are making their names as the school owner pockets the money. The school's proprietor therefore succeeds solely due to their idea that is put into use.

Look around at the big companies, Barclays Bank, Standard Bank, Coca-Cola, Bata Shoe Company, General Motors and Toyota Company. These companies are all over the world but the owners are not known by many, yet many of the best marketers, distributors, managers, deal makers are known in these companies. These people employed by the companies earn a name in what they know and have learnt. They get awards and prices when the company owners make above normal profits. The owners are fully aware that we live amidst people who have talents, gifts, time, money which we can use to benefit ourselves.

Take an example of politicians who buy drinks for the idle youths who go around chanting their name. Politicians know that those around them are natural resources which they can use to their benefit. Ultimately the young people drink themselves silly, the politicians wins the elections only to later disappear till when they need votes again.

Learn that people around you have all you need to get you where you want and move to greater heights in life. They have talents, gifts, time, energy etc but do not know what to do with them. That is why people hawk their gifts from one employer to another. Tap into these waning resources and become rich. The biggest difference between the rich and poor is their position with this secret. The rich know the secret and use others talents, the poor whine of poverty as they hawk their resources. Suit yourself where you think you deserve to be.

8. THE PEN AND PAPER

A pen is an instrument that you use for writing in ink. A paper is a material that consists of thin sheets that you use for wrapping items, writing or drawing. Pen and paper are available to both the literate and illiterate. Over 80% of the people over the world can write and read directly or indirectly. Directly reading means that they themselves can write and read while indirectly means that someone has to do the reading and writing for them.

People who have been to school have been taught how to read and write as well as the basics of surviving through the education systems. Mainly we learnt functional writing of letters, reports, minutes, memos and other communications and looked at the pen and paper as key instruments of communication. Unfortunately after we left the classroom walls we strictly stick to the key essence of paper and pen. We never learnt to look at the pen and paper as resources. When we bought these two items from the canteen, it did not occur to us that they are resources that make someone else rich. Some of the best ideas in the world are recorded on pieces of paper using pens.

Pocket Money

We learn the 26 English alphabetical letters and 10 integers either from home or school. The pen and paper and the 36 symbols equally added makes a difference. Many people have become millionaires by using the above three resources i.e. alphabets and integers, pen and paper.

Put down letters and numbers on a piece of paper, then key them in a computer and you have novels, newspapers, magazines, reports, speeches and more. The composition you wrote about "my first day in school", "my family", "my best teacher", "my country", "how I spent my holiday", "the trip", "when I tasted..." was your training ground. The problem was that no one told you how your composition could earn you billions. The word "composition" is from the word "compose" which means to write music or to produce a piece of writing using careful thoughts.

You learnt how to piece together letters into words, words into sentences, sentences into paragraphs to the required number of words to merit a teacher's nod. What we need to do now is to graduate the paragraphs into chapters, chapters into sections and come up with books and get the book published. Anyone can compose a song or a book in spite of their age. All you need is a mature and critical mind. In any case, you have all the resources that you need around you.

I consider the accomplished businessmen, politicians, industrialists, musicians and all the great people that we know as role models. They may not necessarily be writers, but they have created serene time to craft and document their experiences for all to read. Most bookstores in the world are stocked with inspirational titles of successful businessmen and investors like Donald Trump, Richard Branson, preachers like John Hagee, Joel Osteen, Dollar and politicians like Barrack Obama, Kenyatta and Clinton.

You do not have to be a celebrity or a renowned figure for your book to be read by many. You do not have to be working to pen down your ideas. As a student, a teacher, a cook, house wife, Councilor, Member of Parliament or the CEO of a multinational cooperation, pen on paper your ideas and let others see the world from your perspective. Perception is personal and when we share what we know then our world expands. Be the kind of person that pulls the world from your end and lets other people stretch it.

The list below contains other resources which are available to us in relative amounts. The list is not exhaustive. Consider how different people think of them and how they have used them. How are you using the resources that are readily available at you feet? How can you use them to enhance yourself?

1. Sun and moon
2. Soil
3. Water
4. Earth and universe
5. Air
6. Mathematical signs +, -, x, /

CHAPTER 4

THE POWER OF INTENTION

Pocket Money

Intention is what somebody means to do, a plan or purpose. There is greater force and inertia that imbues a plan or a course. Many times we do things while aiming ahead, without a clear intention or a specific target that guides and acts as a bull's eye.

When football players are on the pitch, their intention is always to put the ball in the net guarded by the opponent goalkeeper. When marathon runners are competing, their goal on the tracks is always to cross the finishing line the first with the fastest time. The goal of gamblers is to outwit the others and take as much money as possible and travelers intend to get to their known destination by a certain time.

Crafting intentions however huge they may be is crucial. Having a clear set goal invites the powers behold in the universe that brings our intentions to completion. This works in line with the law of attraction that states, whatever you focus on grows and comes closer. If you focus on failure then you meet failure and negativity in every corner. If you live positively then you acquire the Midas touch hand and succeed in everything you touch. Even in the dullest of all moments you keep track to reach your intention.

Academics, money, investing, marketing, eating habits, moods, friends, grades, influence and personal factors are one and the same thing. In his book, "Secrets of Millionaires Mind," Harv E. notes that if you save for a rainy day you will surely get a rainy day. Your intention in this case is to save you when an unexpected event happens that requires you to spend. Since you invoked the universe powers to release a rainy day, immediately the universe realizes that you have enough for this task it releases an accident, sickness or a dull moment that requires you to spend some money.

Since you focused on spending on a rainy day a bad day comes and comes three fold. You lose a relative and when returning from the burial you have an accident where one of your sibling breaks a leg.

On the contrary, change your focus on paying more detail on the productive side. Instead of a rainy day save for celebration when you close that deal, when you finish that course or when you enlarge your network. The other day I narrated a childhood experience to my nephew. My siblings left me one day as we headed to school. I chose to use a *panya* route that went through a villagers homestead.

As I was creeping through, a dog came after me barking, I thought I would surely die. I ran as I screamed at the top of my voice. All those present in the compound came out semi naked to see what was causing such havoc so early in the morning. I wanted my nephew to get the picture of how the dog would have attacked me, but he had a different perspective of the story. My nephew was thankful that the dog paced me up so I wasn't late for school. This is what I call optimism.

My nephew focused on me getting to school early before the teacher on duty arrived. He was glad that dogs were on my way to hasten my speed. What seems negative may be placed on our way to push us towards our intended posts. Instead of focusing on what will make us disheartened we should flip the coin and look on the other side. There may be something greater and better than you expect, but if all you look at are the negative sides of your situation then success only becomes a mirage.

It is good to train our children to start doing things with a set target in mind. Help them create intentional goal posts. Let them not go to school from Monday to Friday, week in week out, term in term out without knowing why they are doing it. School should not be just a normal everyday routine, it should be something that is done with a purpose and a clear set agenda. Help your children work with a specific aim in mind. For example, out of 500 marks how many based on the resources you have and commitments can you score in one term. Help them work from the intended target to the individual subjects. For instance, if your child wants to get at least 400 marks out of a possible 500, help them know how many marks are needed from each subject to achieve this. One will probably need 80 marks out of possible 100 per subject.

This way a child identifies the strong subjects that they can score more marks and those that they cannot. This helps the child balance their strengths and weaknesses. Help your child stay on course on the strong points and allocate more time on the weak subjects. Sometimes some students hate some subjects and end up getting poor grades in them. Learning to balance is vital, knowing that life offers us a better side and we also have to live with the bad side.

If your child is not an ardent follower of education, do not be perturbed by the slow pace or low marks they achieve as individuals. Instead congratulate them as they graduate from one intended goal to another. Even if it is of the lowest mark, look at the positive side. Sometimes the child's mind might not have adapted to the education system, but given time they will have a liking to education.

I have a friend who we attended the same high school with. She hated mathematics and could pick an integrated English book or another subject whenever math's teacher came to class. This was her routine from form one to four it was the same story. She scored an overall grade of B constant of 64 points in her KCSE examinations. She had high grades in all subjects except mathematics which she had a D-. She always wanted to pursue law but because mathematics was a compulsory subject she lost the chance by a whisker. The Joint Admission Board (JAB) had her pursue a Degree in Education. She now thumbs chalk as a duty which lies out of her interest. There are possibilities she will still pursue her LLB degree but lack of balancing will still prove costly to her.

While in school, I realized I was good in History but I had to drop it. After registering the first seven subjects required I looked at the others which I required less effort to score high marks. I picked History and Commerce which I always knew would give me twelve points each. I was not a good student in sciences but good subject balancing gave me twelve points. These 24 points gave me a high mileage. I joined the university something that I could not have managed considering the results I used to record in the other school exams.

Education is an area where intentions are vital for young people. Education helps the children to learn how to save with a purpose. Let's say they want a bicycle which costs 3,000/=. Help them learn how to save up to 3,000/= within a particular period. By raising this amount all on their own they will have learnt many other lessons.

First they will have learnt how to suspend a want to a later date. They will know that they can live without something. Secondly they will learn to deal with peer pressure which in most cases has created the urge for them to want to spend what they do not have to. This will happen when they meet their riding colleagues without it and their envy will turn into motivation to cut on other luxuries to purchase the bike. Another life vital lesson is that one should never spend money that they do not have. By enduring for long they realize that one only spends what they have especially for luxury. At a young age, deficit financing can be disastrous.

In most cases that urge to share that particular bicycle or item changes with time. By the time the 3,000/= is collected, their appetite would be for a bigger property largely a liability. Just like in academics the target will create its own energy, time and resources to actualize. A child with a higher aim seeks to add some marks. This way the child wakes up earlier, sleeps late, has only friends that he/she can learn from, borrows books, follows teachers and bother the parents for more time and resources. Therefore, the physics law which states that work creates its own time is obeyed.

The target that you have will always guide you to your intended goal. It is therefore vital to show children the need to forgo some of their luxuries to beef up the kitty. The child may also realize that they may have to sell the toys they have outgrown and at times collect litter in the neighborhood at a fee. Learn to forgo parties but add the money to the kitty. This child will learn the basic money lessons of forgoing one thing for the sake of another that is more beneficial.

A story is told of an old mule that fell into a dip well. The owner had neglected the well and wanted to cover it. The owner on learning the fate of the mule assessed the whole situation and saw no possibility of saving the mule. After thinking for hours he called some of his colleagues to cover the well. He had decided to cover the well with the mule inside since it was old anyway and he wanted to cover the well.

With shovels the mule owner and his friends started covering the well with loose earth. The mule would shake of every other pile of shovel sized earth. Immediately it shook its back, the soil fell under its feet. It did this way with every other soil that hit it from above. With the falling soil forming its base, the mule moved up with every shovel. The mule never got tired of this three hour exercise. The well was soon parallel with the ground and the mule was out of the hole. The mule used what was meant to make it captive to free itself.

Any intention can be achieved if we set our mind to it.
We are all successful failures; in any case no one was born successful. We all have to struggle in one way or another to attain greatness. The mule's intention was to walk free and it did. It endured the successive hit from the soil and soon it was free. It used what was to cover and suffocate it to its advantage. When a focused person is stringent on his/her goals then the onlookers think they are better, advisers and know it all. They laugh at you, intimidate you, slander and smear you with uncouth words. Know this, such people are the narrow roads that lead to salvation. Trying to quickly fix problems with pocket money, first salary or loan may not be the answer.

These negative forces are the shovels of soil the mule endured. With them the mule learnt the patience of a cobra. It was patient for three hours to come out. It never lost hope even though its owner had. Those around you may give up on you like the owner did to the mule. He said it was old and the well was to be covered anyway. To you those around might have told you the same, you are failure, you scored a D- or an E, you are drunkard or useless. Know this the worst mistake you can do is to give up hope on yourself and stop living your life. We all at one point fail in what we are doing. Successful failures pick up from where they did not make it from and move forward, this time however, they are filled with more wisdom.

Pocket Money

What you hear are the words of other minds but not yours. The mule owner might have peeped downwards with his friend, and said, "It can't survive." Little did he know that the mule never heard him as his negativity was countered by the mule's will to live. The mule must have been hopeful up to the top of the hole. What matters is not the depth of the hole we are in, but what we tell ourselves about the hole. The mule must have been thinking of various survival techniques, before it finally gathered the energy to shake the millions of earth particles.

The vital lesson the mule might have learnt throughout the process was, "how to expect the next." After the first few shovels of earth, it must have learnt to expect the next down drudging force with positivism. When you are around scads of negativity, insults and more, learn how to deal with such unconstructive force. The mule took one step up with every shovel and not another scud, more pain, less breath, less fresh air. What are you telling yourself about all you are experiencing, hearing, feeling or going through?

An old adage says, "Obstacles are what you see when you veer your eyes off your target." When you look at how differently we live our lives, you realize how true this is. A student who wants to get the best grades will look at sleep as an obstacle, negative students as obstructions, uncooperative groups as a huddles, lack of pocket money as an obstacle, few friends an obstacle, perturbing teachers as an obstacle, weevil infested *githeri* as obstacle, having to fetch water as obstacle, lack of field trips as obstacle and being a day scholar as an obstacle. He or she will view empty libraries and laboratories as obstacles, not having watched the acted set books as an obstacle, sharing beds as an obstacle, sleeping on a double-decker infested with bed bugs as an obstacle, family violence as an obstacle, not watching football as an obstacle and among many other things.

Our perceptions about what challenges come our way, is what always matters. Being at home gave me a serene environment to do my studies. Not being in school to watch world cup matches on T.V gave me a chance to study. Many are times we blame situations and recede to inaction. Sometimes we blame our parent's inability, our school's inability, the teacher's attitude and government's concern and policy yet all these are external factors. Instead of blaming others for our failures, it is important that we look at our own contributions to our failures.

It is not the teacher's attitude, it is your attitude. It is not the mathematics teacher but the student taking mathematics, it is not my parents, it is about the child born by the parents, it is not the poor economy it is what I am doing as a citizen, it is not about policies it is about what you contributed in the policy, it is not lack of money it is what you have done to lack it. It is always about you, it should be about you and it will always be about you.

Rarely do we usually think or focus on ourselves. At every other moment we are thinking of things, situations external to us. We think of people we love or hate, missed opportunities, failures, successes and focus on helping others so much that we forget the very self. I am not advocating for individualism.
I am only confident that when the self is well taken care of, then taking care of others is more efficient. The principle is simple, place food on your plate and you will see the depression in your neighbor's plate. From there you can share and help level the quantities.

Pocket Money

Much of what occupies us is day's work for employees and studies for those in school. When in the work place there are deadlines that we strive to beat. What we think of is finishing the piece of work, the alarm in the wee hours of the morning, the research, the typing, the organizing, the trip, the pay, and the working environment. All this contributes to us earning a salary at the end of the month.

In spite of all this, we loudly say at the end of the day, "I am tired," "I love my job," "I only work because of the cheque," "if only my boss could know, my salary could be increased." These are socially correct statements which burn the energies more than one can imagine. The society has taught us to always be normal, be it in complaining, appreciating, working, earning, sleeping, dressing, timing or fitting in society. The tendency of normality has turned us into normal complainants.

We never pose to ask ourselves, what direction am I taking? What stakes have I in what I am doing? As an employee sometimes it is about you and not the customer. We have been trained by business owners to know that, 'the customer is key.' Study the popular worker colonizing terms like "customer is key", "the consumer is the employer", "satisfy the customer and you are sorted", "it is all about customer satisfaction", "customer care". If the customer and boss are always right, what about the employee?

Within these highly selling terms in organizations the employee is never mentioned. I have never heard of "employee care", "employee is key". As an employee know that it is all about you before it is the customer. What the business owners have known is that employees are instruments to be used to create undying desire in the customer such that even if they are replaced the customer will still come again. This is done through the flamboyant terms targeting the customer by passing the care (employee).

If employees were to think of whom it is all about, then they would definitely change their position in the businesses.
Employees would probably change their working strategies if they considered themselves as carriers of the missiles that fires. They would change their relations with the customer if they thought the business revolves around their owners and not them. Rarely in our day do we think of how we relate with what we do. If what we do is complain and by the law of attraction we call that which warrants our complaining, this may be about pay, long hours, cladding style, the tea, lunch, heat, computer etc.

As you come up with products, drive vehicles, transport products, offer services, sell products or listen to advertisements, ask yourself what you own. Thinking about all this does not in any way make you jealous or envious. Positioning your mind in this direction is a journey towards success. It is the start of a great soul search that helps us as individuals change our perspective. When we open our eyes and see the bigger picture then we understand our place in organizations. We come to understand the positions that benefit, the work that fulfills and the feeling that actuates.

When we realize that we are a liability to the organization, then we are aware that part of our contract is honored by being indicated in an expense account. Not an account where our efforts, our time, energies and contributions to the organization are recorded. As we learn to accumulate our finances, we realize that getting a job is the first step. Stopping at that is hazardous. Looking ahead is the right way. Decide how many years you wish to be in the organization and how you are improving yourself while in the organization.

Pocket Money

Question if your reasons for working are being met in the organization and if your reason for being employed is met as an employee.

I once met a former college mate in Machakos Town. We exchanged pleasantries and sat at a nearby restaurant to catch up. Two years had long gone before I had seen him. He was now a Chief Executive Officer in one of the Kenyan banks.
It was evident that he loved the experience that he got, the exposure, language, strategy and mentorship. Apparently he started working immediately after college before he had graduated. He worked at several of the bank branches before being promoted to the head office.

However, though he had so much experience in the banking industry he had set himself a time limit to be in the banking profession. Having been in banking for two years, he had three more years to go before he walked away. By the time five years elapsed, he was sure he would have learnt all important aspects that would benefit him. His presence at the bank was threefold, first to learn business tricks in the sector, secondly to network with people in the business world, and lastly to secure a minimum threshold of capital to start his own venture.

Once he was sure he would survive without being employed, he would leave the job. Somebody from outside the sector would say he is settled. But settled is only common to normal employees, normal in the sense that they wake up to work all day or night for a pay cheque for around 30 years and wait for a pension money.

As a student, it is good to understand for what reasons you would want to work. As a young person, it is vital to know that people work for different reasons; majority for money, others for experience, others for strategic positioning, others for networking while others for lack of a better thing to do. It is extremely important to know why you need a certain job. To me knowing why you work is more vital than earning a salary.

While in primary school, I had one teacher whose strictness could not be compared to another. She taught us English for the larger part of my upper primary class. One Friday morning she gave us a passage to read and then do the six exercises that followed in forty minutes. Come Monday morning, none of us had completed the assignment. The assignment seemed too large and too difficult for any of us.

English was the first lesson every Monday morning. Immediately after parade, the English teacher walked in class with a leafy branch of wood. With no words she waved us to lie on the floor. I lay at the back of my seat trembling and shivering in anticipation as blood pulsed through my veins.
One of my classmates was the first one to be chewed on by the leafy branch. I lost count when the strokes got to thirteen.
Before long, the bushy branch was in pieces and scattered on the floor.

Mwendwa the first victim was ordered to bring more strokes from the head teacher's office. With his mind fixed on the strokes he ran into the head teacher's office, went into the inner room and failed to realize that the head teacher was in the office. The head teacher chuckled at the harassed look on Mwendwa's face and said, "*Tengenezweni*," (may you be straightened) teasingly. The English teacher worked on our behinds, from heel to the back of our head. She took off her wrist watch as she quickened the pace. She beat us until she soon took off her jacket, and then what remained was a sleeveless top.

When she was through with the last person she looked at us and said, *"Winakyake ndew'aa kyongi,"* (when you have something of your own you do not accept from others). With these words she picked her jacket and left the room. From this experience I learnt that if you think you are clever then you will rarely accept ideas. Many are times we fail to heed valuable advice because we think what we know is superior to what we are being told. We have superb experiences to learn from but the key lessons go unlearned, we have the best teachers' but then we fail to heed the vital lessons, we have the best preachers but still fail to heed to God's word.

We ignore what other people tell us because we think we are so clever that we cannot absorb any more. We have the perspective that only "fools" go to school. If fools go to school, then to heed good advice is to see you as a fool, to cap what you know. The know it all, know anything. There is arrogance born out of ignorance. The ignorant are defensive but the knowledgeable are humbled by their desire to learn.

In our case the teacher walked away after working on our backs. In reality we would have avoided this pain if only we had gone to ask her or the other teachers for help. She was not punishing us for not finishing our work but our failure to ask her questions. No one in the class had bothered to follow her or any other teacher so she disciplined us for being ignorant.

In real life situations, we pay dearly for the mistakes we commit. We lose our jobs, have our salaries delayed but still stick to the same jobs. Life can be a great teacher when we are foolish. Experience is always the best teacher. If we can set our intention to be learning from the environment, then all we need is in the environment. All the answers are within a certain circumference. Find the radius and reach for it. If one could have one year intention of learning about money then the person would be more knowledgeable about money by the time the year ends. We are not taught about money in school, but still use money. Everyone around us knows a thing or two about money. Seek to know what money is, from the money gurus; learn by asking, associating with them and gleaning from their deeds.

Muturi after completing his college education hustled for a year and first worked as a messenger. He helped his elder friends in River road and mastered the business they were doing. Each of the guys he worked for had printers, computers and electronic machines. His work was mainly to pick orders and execute them. He would print documents and then send them to different parts of the country. Muturi's bosses had contacts countrywide and it was cheap for them to use him to earn.

When customers wanted cards, programs, banners and any other printable articles they would either email or phone Muturi's bosses. Within no time the work is done and sent via email or the commuting vehicles. After working for the first year, Muturi went looking for his own printer which cost 72,000/=.

Knowing that he wanted to be independent, he worked backward. Muturi needed to save 200/= daily for a whole year if he was to buy the printer. By then he had no bank account so he opened an account with Equity Bank. He did not care what was going to happen but he knew a printer was the target.

With this in his mind he became more aggressive. Knowing his salary was 300/= per day he had to re-adjust to survive on 150/= per day. This meant a thirty day working month would provide 4,500/= disposable income in his hands so he tightened his belt. Within a short time Muturi learnt how to design most of the printable graphics. This way he was more valuable to his boss and those around him who had more work or difficulties in designing.

The necessity for survival made him seek more skills not through training but practice using his friends' computers. He saved for a whole year and soon he had accumulated the 72,000/= needed. Muturi rented a room a few meters from his bosses' workshop and since he was always the contact person he had customers from his old workplace. With the new machine and the first 50,000/= worth of contract he began his business.

He marketed aggressively and got his own customers since hustling life had fine tuned him in the social skills arena. Muturi had a sweet tongue so he always convinced his customers. He ensured that he had loyal customers and that efficiency was maintained. Everything was done as scheduled. By caring for his client's needs he made them frequent visitors. By ensuring quality of designs and dexterity of products he attracted more clients.

With the primary customers satisfied and now loyal they become his crusaders and from time to time he could receive calls from people he did not know. Most of his new clients got Muturi's number from print outs or from his loyal customers. The loyal satisfied customers would talk to small crowds about how good his works was.

He was able to secure contacts from larger companies and major event organizers. Everyone marveled at the work that he did. In most cases the organizers never forgot to mention those involved in the success of the particular events. Mainly they would recognize Muturi's business so this way the crusaders had turned into evangelical advertisers. Within two years he had made millions and his business had grown and he had diversified. Muturi had slowly repositioned from hustling to bustling.

Muturi's story highlights the power of intention. Had he just decided to be saving without a specific plan, he would not be rich maybe he would have over 200,000/= in his account but still hustling. Intention is the key word. Have a goal post ahead, and then aim the ball in it. Even if an opponent snatches it from your legs you certainly do not forget the aim, direction and prize to be won after hitting the back of the net.

CHAPTER 5

MONEY AND LIFE CHOICES

Pocket Money

The Macmillan Advanced English Dictionary refers to choice as a range of things that you can choose from. It also refers to the opportunity or right to choose between different things. A study of these definitions shows that things that are to be chosen. It also shows that it is incumbent upon the chooser to identify what ultimately to fall for.

The range of what is to be chosen by every individual is limited to some level. For instance a child in a family has a limited choice up to what is provided for them and their ability to create. The child may think their parents or grownups always have what they want when they want it. The parents are limited to some extent depending on their wealth. Villagers in rural areas may think of those in towns as being affluent. Imagination captures affluence and is limitless to the other position.

Michael Schumpeter said that, "Wealth does not bring happiness but increases the range of choice an individual can choose from".

Having a lot of money doesn't guarantee a sweet life and enjoyable luxury. Happiness is a conscious choice by an individual to being at peace despite their situation. Therefore Schumpeter's argument is true, in that people are happy in the slums while others are crying in posh estates; people are despondent in slums and enjoying in away from the city. Happiness is a choice.

Wealth is defined as a large amount of money and other valuable things or a large supply of useful things. Whoever has more money increases his or her range of choices, for instance the number of toys a child has depends on the amount of money the guardian has. The number of holidays a person has in a year depends on the amount of money one has. The pair of shoes of different hues and shape is determined by the amount of money one has. The number of rooms in a building depends on the amount of money the owner has. The school, college or university one attends is determined by the amount of money one has. The choice of course to pursue is also determined by the amount of money one has, the choice of estate of residence is also determined by the amount of money one has. The much you have determines your range.

Within the range one chooses different stations depending on how much they have.

Range is fluid, just like the amount of money is. Evidence of this plasticity is evident in people's lifestyles at different times of the month and year. Variety is the way at end and start of the month while lack is the common phenomenon mid month. Fluidity is far more evident to overnight millionaires. Those who win lotteries or promotions largely usually do not hold on to their wealth for long. With higher incomes the choice continuum extents shuttering previous limits. Blown out of balance the overnight millionaire is tempted to change diet, company, pub, estate, stop working, consuming more than he/she can sustain in the long term.

T. Harv. Ecker says the reason why lottery winners usually do not keep their money for long is because their money blue print is set to handle low amount. So they have to waste away to amounts they can handle comfortably. The best way to do this is to spend more to assume a higher status only manageable for long in their imagination.

With financial advice, instant large sum winner's can suitably adjust their financial blue print to reflect the money they have acquired. In the same way instant paupers swing from one end to the other of the choice continuum. In most cases they swing from wider range of choices to lesser. Choosing what to pick in times of affluent choices is more willed, the other way round is more forced. Sometimes people are forced to choose between the lesser of two evils i.e. Kibera or Mathare slum residents may be asked to forgo tomato or onion in meals, to pay school fees for a child or buy them food or clothes, tooth paste or tooth brush.

With dwindling range of choices people lose their freedom. When the variety is one that you must choose from then you are no longer free but become a slave. You easily lose your ways and follow what you have to choose ways.

A story is told of a hunter who hatched his grand plan of hunting. He thought of first owning a dog. He could not get a fine mature trained dog so he decided to raise a puppy and bring it up for months. When the dog was strong enough with a differentiated smell he debuted into the bushes. After several corners of brushing shrubs a warthog was awoken from deep slumber and led the way.

The hound chased the warthog with the dog owner trailing from behind. Within five minutes both the hound and the warthog were out of the hunter's sight. Keenly he followed the paws and hoofs of the animals. As he walked he came to a point with two pavements. There the warthog hoof marks went one way and the dogs paws followed gazelle like hoofs on the other pavement. The dog owner became disappointed but still followed the pavement with his dogs' marks.

After a while he found a bushy shrub with one side the gazelles hoof marks and the other antelope like (smaller) hoof marks being followed by his dog paw marks. With this he became more despondent but decided to follow the hoofs and paws. This time expecting a smaller kill he was still hopeful of some meat. He followed the pacing dog faster, but found himself slower due to fatigue. About two corners he found the path the animals had been following had branched.

This time the hoofs his dog followed had become smaller. More so they were those of a dik dik, with those of the antelope walking un-escorted. This trend continued until he came to an aunty hill where the hound was sniffing the underground tunnels with the whole entrance marked by rat paw marks.

With all the animals on the chase having left the hook, the hound was palpitating and heavily panting, gasping air but with no kill. All the tributary points of his following the hound, stood a mile away. It seemed a heavy task for him to chase the animal all by himself. In the end he had no catch and bigger animals had escaped him and seemed a distant away. The dog was tired and needed some help home.

Even though the hunter had a big well fed and trained dog, it could not feed him with the game meat that he needed. Many people have entered into lifestyles which cannot feed them, protect them or house them. Just like the hunted animals stood a mile away from the hunter, many of the choices people hope for appear a distant away. The choices seem distant even after earning a salary fully worked for (dog) and the salary cannot help you really do the choosing. The salaries you get seem to relegate you to items of lesser value, residence of greater insecurity, residence which is water deficient. Just like the dog seemed to lead the owner to a smaller animal. People's earnings seem to relegate them to lesser value choices.

It is important for any student or person to know that the amount of money they have or will have determines the extent and intensity of choices at their disposal. It is money that enlarges the size of the blanket to cover more, it is the numbers that lengthens the radius of the umbrella to cover more from rain drops and sun rays. Remember, it is more of variety and not contentment. Plenty doesn't mean you are enjoying like earlier alluded, happiness is a conscious choice you make despite the surrounding.

It is important to have an informed choice before deciding on something. This implies that an individual matches ahead on a road he or she knows its breadth and depth. As we choose what to do in order to earn money, we should bear in mind about a careers ability to give more for wider choices. Even as our parents facilitate our moving into different careers our choices largely depends on what they have. If they have more, the drape of choices would be longer.

Many of us found ourselves in careers that do not give room for a variety of the choices. It is upon us to choose which way to go. With internet technology, distance learning and part time classes, one can enlarge their base of skills. My employer at one time advised us on widening our base in order to survive. Ask yourself what you can do to broaden your career. Realize what most people do and earn money from what you have learned.

It takes patience and a clear conscious mind to absorb a skill. Learn as much as you can, acquire skills, interact with diverse crowds and your choice plate will always be wide. With a high dexterity of skill then the amount of what you earn increases with every skill you put into use. In addition to having more to do, make sure that you can choose what to do. You are not likely to go wrong in your practice if you have many skills. In the end you are likely to do more of what is close to your heart. The greatest of all professions is that which lifts a downtrodden spirit, that which puts a smile on a sad face, more so to the professor than to whom it is professed. The choice of such people is confined to doing well to all and hence their choice of who to serve is wider hence lacking money is not an issue.

Widening our bases is a choice that depends on the amount of money one has. On the flip side, widened bases are more stable and bring in more money hence widening the spectrum of choices further. Limitation is not about limited resources, it is more on limited imagination and usability of natural endowments like hands, legs etc.

Employing is choosing what is usable in an individual. Choosing a career is about elevating and developing one area of self for use while suppressing others. People choose to earn from a limited use of their mouth, athletes use their legs to win millions, writers earn through their hands, teachers get more money through their mouths and dancers get an extra coin by moving their bodies. The idea is activating parts of the body to do many things. The hands are able to do so many things; therefore an individual who trains his or her hands to perform various tasks widens his range of choice at his disposal.

The person who trains his or her mouth to serve many activities is far much better, e.g. eat, cheer, jeer, teach, sing and entertain. The person who is able to do many things has widened his or her choice of tasks and can perform at any time. Such an individual can be in a cheering squad, choir and benefit self in other ways hence increasing ways of earning.

To train different parts of the body to perfection requires coaching or copying. The range of skills that one can train is numerous, but still depends on the amount of money available or ones imagination. The wider the range of skill for a particular body part the higher the amount of money you can earn. Some of the skills which are highly rewarding may not require going to school but depend on personal will. Some uses of body parts are invented by individuals. One therefore doesn't have to sit in class to be taught how to use the mouth to entertain but practice and self identify the use of body parts. How else can you use all your body parts profitably with the least cost?

The objective of a master is to limit the choices of the enslaved; the colonialists knew this too well. Their way of limiting options to all who they colonized made them stretch their rule for many years. Another role of the master is usually to censor whatever the slave has access to. This way all the choices at the slave's disposal favor the master. The slave is controlled like a marionette by the master. The slave only laughs when tickled by the master and dances when the beat reigns.

With money you control the options at your disposal. You soften hard surfaces and flatten hills to ant hills. With money you are able to be the master and not the slave and you are able to determine for how long your choices are useful. When the taste to the slave changes, the slave has no choice but to content with what is available. When the taste of the master changes he seeks to be contented somewhere else because he has a large pool to choose from.

Chapter 6

THE POCKET MONEY EQUATION (INCOME EQUATION)

Pocket Money

The relationship between the money we earn and spend can be summarized in an equation. Many students usually find mathematics challenging but it is important that you understand this particular equation;

$$Y = C + T + S + N$$

Where; Y= All your earnings. To a student all pocket money.

C= Part of the income is spend in consumption. This is the fraction of your income that sustains you.

T= is what the government deducts as taxes from salaries. For students, it is the pocket money since they have no salaries they pay through purchase of products and services.

S= is the amount of Y that remains after you have consumed. The government has taken its share through taxes. Generally S is what one saves.

N= stands for money you give away to charity, as tithe, offering, *zakat* which are not tax, consumption or saving.

In economics other items are usually added to the income equation. For example in the computation of national income, additions of money send abroad and received from abroad is between total imports and exports. At an individual level we work with the equation **Y= C+S+T+N**

In the next chapters we focus our attention to each of these items.

Chapter 7

Y- INCOME

Pocket Money

Y represents the income from other sources but it varies from one person to another. In the case of students, income could be termed as the pocket money they get from various sources. No parent or guardian tells the students what to do with the pocket money they give them. Employees line up in banks every month so income is the payment for work done. This is money that comes into an individual pockets. Income refers to all that an individual is entitled to get even before any coin is subtracted. Before the government takes its share, before you consume part of it, before you put some aside then that gross total is ascribed to you.

Sources of Income
Money experts agree that there are two types of incomes, namely:
i. Active income
ii. Passive income

Active income is what is earned after working. It is what people receive in form of wages after working or the salary every end month. One does not get active income if they do not work. Though agreed upon before work commences, the worker gets the income after he or she satisfies the employer's demands. Getting active income is what the larger mass depends on. Education systems train people to earn salaried jobs. It is what we are all channeled to. We are born, enjoy going to school and complete college then start hunting for jobs. We hustle, tarmac and wane in search of jobs. We do not tarmac because we want employment, but because we are looking for money.

Having a job is one channel of having money in our pockets. Students earn their income when parents and guardians give them money pegged on a task. Having money for students should not be limited to being given some coins. Creativity is key. Students may not be in a conducive environment for earning money, but a creative mind prevails.

Passive income is the money an individual earns without working. It includes money given as pocket money for students, rent from leased property, dividends from shares owned, interest etc.

This money is not dependent on any amount of work done but invested moods of the giver, day of the month and shrewdness of the investor. I choose to classify pocket money under passive income because the giver – never in most cases– expects much from the receiver. Parents never have pre- conditions when giving pocket money to their children. In most cases, giving pocket money is an obligation with no set limits which the receiver is not required to account for.

Sources of Pocket Money
1. Being given: We give pocket money and our children receive. This is one source where it is assumed one may need to buy something extra for themselves. The amount given depends on the giver or sometimes the shrewdness of the receiver.

A friend of mine, Eric, shared how he gives his daughter pocket money. Eric visited his daughter every week after opening and gave her 500/=. This was a routine despite him giving her money before she reported for school. In addition, Eric and his wife developed a competition between themselves over who loved their daughter more. They would both try to outdo each other in the amount they gave her.

In such a situation the daughter finds herself with money she has not worked for or money with no direct use in sight. Such surplus steady income to a non-working student teaches something. One learns that if you fail to work, those who love you will give you money. In the real world this is not true.

In Eric's case, conflicts between him and his wife gives their daughter a destruction tool with no manual for use.

It is common for parents to give extra money on top of school fees, fare and for personal effects to their children. In the mind of the giver this money is for just "incase" something goes wrong. In case they have to purchase something; siblings too give the one going to school money. Those in school have learnt to expect some money from those around them i.e. uncles, cousins, or grandparents. The children sometimes question why they are not being given money.

Students receive money by both friends and foes for many reasons and at times for no reason. Friends would give the money to portray they cherish their friendship while foes would give money to win the enemy back or soften their hearts. Strangers also do give money to school going students for various reasons, i.e. get sexual favors or other favors from them or to help in a certain plans.

In a certain school there was a drug syndicate involving students and villagers. The main drug being sold was bhang. A villager gave a day scholar one thousand shillings and the boy was soon intoxicated with the money though he knew nothing about the drug. Soon, the boy was the villager's distributor within the school. The villager would go around harvest and package it, and then the student would carry it on his way to school. The day scholar was not a bhang or cigarette smoker but with a thousand shillings each week he peddled drugs into the school.

Matatu touts are known in Kenya for seducing young school girls. With their flashy life and notes on their fingers like rings, they easily win the hearts of school girls. The money from the touts makes school girls more gullible hence are preyed and attacked. What the girls may not know is that the money doesn't belong to the touts but to the owner of the *matatu.*

Teachers, tutors, lecturers too give students money for various reasons. Teachers may give their students money in exchange for a task done or for sexual favors.

Pastors too give money to students and other people either genuinely or with disguised reasons. The society trusts the people of God. With all this trust bestowed on one person, many people become easy prey for foxes in sheep's skin.

2. *Sponsorship/scholarship:* Many scholarships and sponsorships given to students are inclusive of upkeep allowances. Other sponsorships include tuition fee or partial sponsorship of the tuition fee. Those scholarships that provide full sponsorship including allowance, meals, accommodation and even personal effects that tends to be destructive to the receiver. They entirely teach a lesson which is unrealistic to the world.

During my primary education a certain Non-Governmental Organization came in our area to provide educational support for the needy children. The organization provided uniform to the children, school fees and all other dues owed to them, shoes, personal effects including food back home. In fact, sponsored children were the only ones who wore shoes in the whole school. Others brushed grass along pavements to school. They were also provided with training equipment on Saturdays with all nice facilities i.e. balls, sport shoes and nets. To top it all up, the beneficiaries of the organization got a trip once a year to places of their choice.

Every other growing child envied the sponsored ones. The promise of being sponsored to whatever level a child wanted made the package more enticing. The organization's promise was, "We will fuel your steps and oil your way. When you sleep we sleep first." It is rather unfortunate to report that over 70% of students sponsored in the decade spanning from 1990-2000 dropped from primary school, 25% in their secondary school and 5% that went through secondary education, only 1% managed to go to the university. The only known university sponsored was one person but he performed poorly in KCSE, stayed out for two years then went back when he qualified.

The unfortunate thing with sponsorships is that they cushion the children from major life lessons. I wish the package included more than just "fuel" through the program. The students, who failed to get sponsorships, wore torn uniforms, no shoes, were frequently being chased from school and did not go for school trips did better than the sponsored students. They got high grades, completed school in larger percentages and become more responsible citizens.

Let us not choose lifestyles that cushions us from pain meant to drive in us life lessons of endurance, perseverance and creativity. We were once asked to come with a 30cm ruler the following Monday by the Mathematics teacher. I was sure I would not ask my parents to buy the item for me. Since I had to spend the whole of Sunday herding cattle I thought of carving. I decided to curve my ruler. On arriving at school I picked my friend's ruler and used it to calibrate mine. When the teacher came to class I was safe. For him he went home and picked from the provided facilities. My creativity and

103

want made me think and tick. In the end my friend dropped from school and I completed my education.

I am not in any way against scholarships and sponsorships. I greatly acknowledge their role in shaping lives and their contribution to society besides giving hope to the hopeless.
As a student, you must be responsible and find a way of using disposable income from scholarships. Find out other channels that you can responsibly use your pocket money.

3. *Working:* Another source of pocket money is through working. Many students are forced to work to get school fees and pocket money. Given a choice, many would choose to be given pocket money without working. Work is the task that a person does to attract a pay. The pay would vary from place to place and task to task. Work could be within their home or outside their homestead.

Tasks for which the family could employ an outsider could be done by the child. These tasks include cleaning the vehicle, repairing a bicycle, fencing, farming, herding cattle during the weekends or holidays, mowing grass and cleaning the compound. These are tasks requiring some realm of the child's experience and skills. Even if the student is not for the idea, it could be put in such a way that it is similar to their idea. Let not the student think that you are employing them. Sometimes parents demean the work to a class below their children. Some parents cannot allow their children to do any menial duty like washing their clothes or their house. Looking back how I used to make pocket money, I would say I learnt more than just money.

A friend back in school ploughed people's *shambas* as a way of raising pocket money. Another would fetch water using their bulls for functions and get paid. Our dear friend James who used to have more money would work with a tractor and get lots of money. Through treacherous means he would defraud his parents' income.

Working teaches us more than we expect. Within the city or town setting the chances for students working still exists. Students could offer car washing services in their estate, clean the environment, clean neighbor's window panes and trim grass at a fee. Be creative and think of ways of solving people's problems at a fee.

The idea of working for ones pocket money instills more work values in personal growth and development. It is hard for a person who has learned to be creative while in school to suffer or hustle for many years after school. Creativity incorporated with the freedom to work and earn in a larger scale helps a person. In the attempt to provide the best to our children we cushion them from pricks that taught us and molded us. In the end we make life simple for them to learn the hard lessons. Caution should accompany all forms of upbringing.

4. *Allowances:* This is the money that the students are entitled to, by virtue of behaving or being in a certain way. Allowances could come inform of a reward scheme based on merit and teach the student particular lessons.

The rewarding scheme could come in form of birthday gifts. Graduating from childhood behaviour to a mature one e.g. a child who stops bed wetting, keep the nose clean and make their bed could be given some money. Caution should be given to this practice. It is always vital to graduate from material rewards like money, presents to more abstract, presents like praise in each of the behaviors being instilled. The reason is that too much familiarity looses meaning.

5. *Sale of belongings*: As a person grows from childhood to a student, they find they have accumulated many things. Mostly a student outgrows toys, clothes, dolls and other belongings. With permission from their parents the student or pupil can sell these belongings in order to raise some money.

The other day, I paid a visit to my brother. His children –my nephew and niece– took the cookies that I had with me. My nephew of about 9 years decided to sell his share of cookies. From prior learning he had learnt that cookies are friendly to toothache. The cookies got divided into two. His sister ate and finished hers and was soon crying for her brother's cookies.
He went to their mum, counted and multiplied the cookies by five shillings each. He had successfully made thirty shillings and he told his father how his sister's appetite had made him "rich."

The African culture teaches us how to give and receive. It is rare to visit a house with children empty handed. If you lack anything that can be eaten, then it is more African to give them some money. Children should exploit this and keep such money and convert the gifts they receive into money.
Accumulating is the way to go. It would be a vital lesson to learn that it is only at their age they can receive money without working for. Even beggars in town usually master the art of appealing to the sympathies of others which is a trade.

My nephew had learned how to convert what he did not need into savings. He would sell cookies to his sister and bill his father. His father was the bank. Every time he sold something to his sister; he waited for his dad and ask him to add the money to his account. From time to time he would ask to see all his money, count it and then return it.

6. Business/Trade: Many pupils or students start engaging in business in their life. Some realize what the others need then create or provide it at a cost. Trade within primary and secondary schools may not be allowed. Even within the set guidelines, there are things the school cannot object to the students doing.

While in primary school during different fruit seasons, many pupils would come with the fruits and sell them. The trade in most cases attracts suspension from school. There are some items that most pupils consume, which if well invested in can be a source of pocket money. In high school, many girls are known to be masters of hair plaiting. Since all the girls yearn for beauty, then it becomes a market for you. Volunteer in salons if you lack this skill during the holidays. This way you learn the art of hair and nails and how to make money in the process.

Young men can also start their own *kinyonzi* though purchasing required materials for the business could cost you some little amount. If you do not know how to shave volunteer in a *kinyozi* and learn the trade. The idea is to know your colleagues' desire then fill the existing gap.
Doing business while in college is easier. This is because the restrictions regarding businesses are less stringent and the number of people is higher. One may not necessarily start the business in school or college but it is easier to get the capital needed to start any business. University students get loans which they can use to start businesses with.

Things we learn to make while in school could be in demand. For example, you learn how to make incubators in college but stopping at learning would be a life mishap. Start making your own incubators and put them up for sale. If you identify that a particular product will be needed later in future then it will be beneficial if we provide the item at a fee.

Timetables in many colleges allow students the flexibility to do business. Part time students having classes one day a week or evening classes have more time. Full time students usually have their lessons well spaced to give room for flexibility. Remember you do not have to be a part timer. Time is an artificial concept that is created. Play with it to your advantage.

Within the universities doing business is more possible. Any lucrative business is possible for university students. The market is ever present to a willing business mind Find that which the mass like and charge them for it. Shorten the distance they use, fuel their life, cook for them or be their grocer. This is all possible only if you are alert.

A story is told of Florence who after being in the university for a year realized the dress code among university students. She went through her savings but soon realized that she had insufficient funds to start a clothing business. By the end of the first year she had learned the university system. She realized that the signing of the nominal roll can be delayed till some days to exams. She also got to know that most university students had access to their HELB loan within the first two weeks.

With this knowledge, she borrowed money from other students, left for Dubai, bought clothes with their money and sold to them. Since in most universities classes are not compulsory and could take a month before they started, being away for two months wasn't interfering with Florence's studies. Within the first two months of every semester Florence would leave for Dubai, bring clothes, sell them all and settle for two months in class.

By the time she was finishing her education, Florence had already ventured in real estate and land development business. This separated her from the park of university graduates.

7. *Stocks:* Students at different levels also choose to play the game of stocks. They venture in it using tuition fees, savings, borrowing money from friends and relatives. The world of stocks is so dynamic; unless you create interest it will appear strange. Some young people join university when they already have stocks, others may not know and may never know about them.

While in college an article published by the university press read, "The Millionaire Within". It was the story of a third year university student who invested in stocks while still a freshman. His mother had seen his son's interest on the stocks. The young man decided to invest his HELB loan and savings of twenty thousand in the stock market. His mother gave him an additional 100,000/= and he invested the 120,000 in stocks. The man bought and sold his stocks again and again. By the time the article was being published three years down the line, he had stocks worth over a 1 million shillings.

Therefore, consider stocks as another way of not just getting pocket money but also a channel of earning a living and becoming wealthy.

Chapter 8

CONSUMPTION OF POCKET MONEY

Pocket Money

In our basic equation, the income (earned or acquired pocket money) is used as consumption first. Our basic definition of consumption includes the money we use to feed ourselves, cloth, drink, rent, transport, offering and alms. It is what you spend on and is not expected to give you money in return. We are all consumers even before we start earning. Part of a student or pupil's income supplements their parents' budget on them. The pupil or students pocket money is part of the parents or guardians consumption since they are their dependents.

Pocket money could be consumption expenditure on the giver but income to the receiver. The receiver receives much of pocket money without instructions on how to spend it. It is upon the receiver –in many cases students and pupils– to choose how they want to consume a fraction of their pocket money. The money allocated to this vote of spending is the largest.

Things Many Young People Spend Their Pocket Money On:

1. Edibles: One chooses what to eat and determines how many times they eat and the amount of money that they spend on edibles. This could be food, drinks and beverages etc. School meals are available to students, so most of students choose to strictly eat school meals and save their pocket money.

Others choose to consume more food from the school canteen and less from the school kitchen hence saving little or not saving at all. Some students get so broke in the middle of the term and feign sickness to go home and get more. At the university and college, students choose to cook in their hostels or eat from the campus hotels available. What you choose to eat and where you choose to eat from, determines how much you spend and save. Preparing your own meal in the hostel has proven to be more efficient and successful.

Primary school children also have a choice to make on how they spend the little amount given to them. For them, it is a choice between an insatiable desire for sweets and what appears exotic. Highly hyped lifestyles consume more hence the consumption docket of what we have with us. A bottle of 500ml soda costs different prices at different corners of town. A cup of tea costs different at different places in town but it could cost even less to cook it for one self.

2. Clothes: Choice of cloth and place of purchase also affects the price though the quality may be the same. Branded cardigans tend to cost more than plain ones. Choice of new or second hand also affects the amount we spend on clothes. Time of purchase; end month, mid month, rainy season will also affect the price. To spend less on clothes, choose the market, decide the type of cloth you want new or old and time of the month or year.

3. Personal effects: These are items that are vital for upkeep. They may not be seen by anyone as you walk, talk and perform your duties but may affect confidence levels. They include toothbrush, toothpaste, soaps, phone, pen, handkerchief, towel, mattress, sheets, bed covers, undergarments, rings, earrings, bungles, necklaces, wrist watches, clocks, wall hangings, bags and hangers and many more.

Quality does determine the price of an item. When buying anything try and consider the price of the item in as much as quality also matters. Carry out a survey to compare the prices of what you need.

4. Paying fees/dues: Some students usually use their pocket money for payment of dues in school. Others will never use their pocket money to pay an amount they can afford. Students go home to collect two hundred shillings after paying five hundred shillings as their fare home. Some calculative students pay the amount and maybe bill the guardian or parent later.

5. *Trips:* A number of times students go for field trips or visit other institutions, natural monuments, game parks or friends. In such cases, students are required to raise money for these tours. Money collected by the students through fund raising helps them advance social skills. In cases when a student is not able to raise or get money from parents or guardian one can use the pocket money that they have.

6. *Giving:* This includes offering and tithes in the church, contributions towards sickness, death or helping the unfortunate. The amount one chooses to give affects what remains. This goes out of your pocket as consumption in our earlier equation. Benevolent contributions are common where people gather. They appeal to the sympathies of others for help. Within larger gathering, this has been used to defraud the unwitting. Some people are known to kill everyone in their family for the sake of collecting funds. Giving and not giving may not make any difference in your personality.

Consumption item includes all expenditure on items, services and goods and contributions that decrease the amount of money one has.

Chapter 9

SAVINGS AND POCKET MONEY

Pocket Money

Part of the pocket money is usually saved by the student or an individual. Savings is a larger part of what remains after consumption. Most students while in primary and secondary school do not have bank accounts. In fact most of those who qualify for university only open bank accounts in anticipation of the HELB loan. Some students proceed to complete their degree courses without adding a single cent to the account apart from the loans they receive every semester.

The largest percentage of high school and primary school students store their pocket money in their boxes, trousers or with certain teachers and school bursars. This money is not safe as it can be lost, used or stolen. Most children do not trust their money with their siblings or their parents. Students believe if their parents keep their money then come the next term their pocket money will be rationed, or given part of what is banked for them. This makes them bank in their boxes, pockets or they are motivated to spend all.

These are the formative years for a growing mind and whatever they pick as they grow is hard to drop as they age. When students choose their teachers as their banks, there is the danger of an intimate relationship growing or the student misusing the money. Some teachers are also intimidated by the money that their students have. A high school teacher said there was a particular female student who came to school with more money than he earned in a month. The student was a Sudanese refugee staying in Kenya. The United Nations gave her 20,000/= for her up keep. This amount was provided to those above 18 years. After paying school fees she would be left with a lot of money. The student trusted this male teacher so she could have him bank the money for her every term. At the end of the term she could give him a commission of 2,000/=.

To the detriment of the student, the teacher lost objectivity in assessing the particular student. Her grades dwindled and she failed to perform well. Learning to save at a tender age is vital in life. Saving doesn't mean one learns to be stingy or becomes a miser. Saving means keeping part of what one has for future use. It also hinders one from misusing the money in unplanned ways. Therefore, it is extremely vital for parents, guardians, friends and relatives to help our students and young people keep some money, shirts and clothes for the future.

While in form three and four, our commerce teacher advised us to gently wash our shirts as we would need them in the future. Back home after high school, I had no clothes to wear other than my uniform. I realized the usefulness of the uniform. I learnt a vital lesson from my commerce teacher, it is important that we put aside what we do not need now for future use.

Many people in life are caught in groups that are trying to fill certain gaps. These gaps have been created by marketers in you and enforced by friends and peers. Many students and pupils exist in groups that lack a sense of direction. If the group is doing one thing it becomes hard for the group members to break the yolk, compliance is called. Discipline doesn't lie in complying with what the group says, it is being able to abide by your own set directions.

Choosing to buy something because your friends are buying is becoming normal. Normal means doing what others are doing. You become an average student then an average college student, later an average hustler and an average hand to mouth worker if all you do is abide by the rules of other people. If you become an average citizen because of your own doing then your life will be filled with incessant struggles.

A sure way of saving for a student is looking at the C-consumption and reducing consumption hence increasing the amount saved. Realize that you can eat more healthy foods cheaply. You can shine on cheap cardigan. Remember, it is the 'how' and not the 'what' that counts.

Chapter 10

TAXES

Pocket Money

Our equation Y=C+S also includes taxes represented by T. Hence the equation is Y=C+S+T. Students also usually pay taxes. Every year in the month of June a statement about Value Added Taxes (VAT) is made. These are taxes we pay through our purchase of goods and services. Students usually buy goods when they shop and purchase services like transport.

In general terms the T is added to the equation especially on salaried individuals and companies. The salaried are deducted even before they get their monthly pay. Companies and institutions are also taxed. Tax on the salaries of individuals lowers the amount available to the individual. An individual's salary less the tax element is referred to as disposable income. The amount of money that remains after one has paid bills will be lower than the initial salary before taxation.

Companies and institutions pay taxes as per the profits accrued. Governments taxes salaries and profits of companies in order to provide more services and infrastructure for a nation's development. When citizens pay their taxes, a country increases its revenue hence improves services and public goods. On the other hand if the government is corrupt then the public money disappears into private and selfish projects. That is why everyone as young as they are should be vigilant on the use of their taxes. The biggest sin you can commit is to keep quiet when your sweat is wasting away in frothy pockets.

Although students may not have companies, may not be salaried and may not pay taxes, it is vital for them to understand the tax concept. Know the weight inform of taxes that you have to shoulder. The best way to negotiate a corner is to know it, know the way of taxes and how to evade taxes legally. As you grow and study the PAYE – Pay As You Earn schemes. If you are keen, you realize that taxes increase as the salaries grow. It is good to know this and seek an alternative ladder to lean on.

All ladders lean on some walls but the gradient varies from one to the other. We choose ladders that drain us rather than help us move up. Being an employee is one way taxes drain our efforts as we move up. Taxes make an employee crawl through life instead of flying. Taxes tie us closer to the base and wet our wings.

As a boy I remember the traps we used to set up in order to catch birds. Our home area is a dry place so birds depend on people's homesteads for water. We therefore kept water in drums to attract the birds. We would then set the drum in an open area and hide in some safe distance with a cover. The unsuspecting birds would patch around the drum entrance then drop in one by one. As soon as they dropped in the drum, we would prance and cover the entrance.

We would then roll the drum round with the caged birds inside. This made the birds wings wet hence even after taking the cover away no bird would escape. This way we would collect the birds of all types, male and female then break their wings as the last control measure. To date, I still yearn for the weaver birds' roasted meat.

Just as I yearn for the birds' meat, so does the government yearn to enlist you as a tax payer. Tax is the cage the government would wish to cage everyone in and the cage everyone would wish to cage out. But all in all, paying taxes is what strengthens an economy.

Chapter 11

INVESTMENT (I)

Pocket Money

In our equation Y=C+S+T, income is being consumed, saved and taxed. When we consume (C) the money changes hands and it no longer belongs to us. The money we are taxed (T) is no longer ours but the government's. We only see where it is invested in but do not enjoy it directly. It is spend on what individuals cannot provide for themselves. The part of saving remains ours but further away from us.

We need to ask ourselves, where does the money go? Why do banks and shylocks talk of interest? How else can I think of the money under my name? Economists usually equate savings to investments an individual makes. Therefore the money you have in the bank is your investment, if not it is declining in value. It would qualify to be an investment because its outcome is a function of time, entrepreneurial skills and rate of interest. Therefore we have our simple equation:-
Savings (S) = Investments (I). This means that in our original equation Y= C+S+T can be Y= C + I + T.

Savings are counted as investment because saving to invest later and borrowing to invest are similar but inverse. In the first instance, one chooses to accumulate small amounts in the bank for future use. This future could be an investment, while the money in the bank could be earning some interest. This means you withdraw the principle amount plus earned interest from the bank.

While the amount in the bank is borrowed by another person or business, the bank invests it on your behalf. This represents the second instance, where a client borrows and uses the money for some time therefore creates more money. One would do this at an interest rate. This means that the client who borrowed the money will pay the principle and the interest. This is more similar to when you are the one giving the bank money to keep it on your behalf.

The differences lie in the following areas.

Giving The Bank Money	Borrowing From The Bank
No limit to amount you can deposit.	There is a limit you can borrow.
Interest earned is low.	Interest paid is high.
Delays start of a project awaiting the required amount to hold.	Client starts project first then pays as the project matures.
One saves from work.	The investment once stable pays its own principal and interest.
Investing in seasonal and immediate opportunities is hard since money saved may not be enough.	It is easy to borrow from a bank and invest in passing opportunities.

Chapter 12

CASE
STUDIES

Pocket Money

These are highlighted stories from the news and internet that
point out to the fact that those who succeed in due
time are those who open their eyes and remain focused.

1. 16 Year Old Student Is Named CEO Of The Year
   (A story by Erick Ochieng of Standard Media, on
   21/10/2010 Junior Achievement)

Kenya's Humphrey Munga Rogoma, a form three student at
Lenana high school beat students from 13 other countries to
win the coveted prize.

How would you feel to be voted by an entire African continent
as chief executive officer (CEO) of the year? For 16 year old
Humphrey Munga Rogoma, a form three student at Lenana
High School, Nairobi, it was a dream comes true. Rogoma who
heads Man and Company which manufactures and sells
scarves to parents, teachers and students was voted by Africa
as the top most CEO last week. He beat contestants from 13
African countries at a continental competition staged at
Kenyatta International Conference Centre in Nairobi. Junior
Achievement (JA), organized the competition in partnership
with Citi Bank.

Special Ceremony
Rogoma was later feted at a special ceremony at Citi Bank's
headquarters in Nairobi which was presided over by Francisco
Vanni and D' Archirafi, World JA Executive Board Member,
and Citi Bank's Global Transaction Services CEO.

Apart from the trophy and fame, Rogoma received a laptop
and a blackberry phone among other prizes. "We settled on
scarves because it is a warm attire for students who brave
chilly mornings going to school," said Rogoma. Who said he

would pave the way for another person to head the company made up of 35 students next year so that he can concentrate on his end year final exams. The company beat two other schools during regional competitions that propelled them to the continental champions.

Four Other Awards

Apart from winning the overall award, the company also scooped the Kiongozi (CEO), Faidha (profits and dividend), Ujuzi (creativity) and Adihi (responsibility) awards. "Heading a company is not easy. I learnt to be a good listener, tolerant and purpose- driven. I have also mastered leadership skills that is helpful in managing people", said Rogoma. JA is a world forum that teaches, students including those in universities, entrepreneurship, financial literacy and readiness for work.

From Humphrey Rogoma's story you realize that it is never too early to create and run a company. The dictionary defines a company as an organization that provides services or produces goods to meet public needs. I define it as a conglomeration of individuals working with raw materials to satisfy people's needs. With your colleagues, you can identify a problem, gap or a need and solve it at a cost that is higher than the cost of production hence a profit.

A lucrative area would be the science congress, drama and music innovations by students. Once these activities come to an end the enthusiasm is lost in book concentration. If the institution is blind to these routine ventures as a student do not forget it is your life and you are in school for a limited duration. Find other avenues to nurture your potential and talents.

Pocket Money

I once taught in a school that had the undying talent for one student. The school was known to have the ability to move masses musically. During one festival the students misbehaved and music concerts and participation was shelved from the school activities. This move demoralized the students greatly. One of the students during holidays decided to record music in Nairobi. I was impressed by the talent exhibited in her songs. Within the school she could steal every opportunity to practice and lead others in song and dance.

The institution you are in may not support your talent and may disregard you while protecting the other students. The 2010 elected Makadara Member of Parliament, Gideon Kioko Mbuvi alliance Sonko, said that he earned his first million when he was in form two. Approximately a form two student should have been about 16 years. By 16 years he was in business deals with his father which sharpened his money wits. He learned from his father. Do not say that you have no deal maker to learn from, look around you and you will learn all you want. All you need is around you just reach for it.

Humphrey Rogoma was recognized as a CEO at 16 years; Kioko Mbuvi (Sonko) made his million at about 16 years old. How old are you? Have you become a CEO yet? Have you made your first million?

2. She Built Millions from a Sh30 Loan
(Adapted from Daily Nation of 24/11/2010 by Julius Sigei)

After completing form four, she borrowed money to buy kales. This set her on her long journey to success. Anyone who saw the tall slender girl just out of high school sell groceries at the Bomet Municipal Market eight years ago may not recognize her now.

Having started off with borrowed vegetables worth Ksh.30, which she sold for Ksh.60, she is now a reputed supplier of food to various institutions in the region. The third born in a poor family of eight, Ms. Yael Mutai's star dimmed further when, in the middle of her Kenya Certificate of Secondary Education Examination, she was informed that her father had died.

"It was devastating. I had always been sure that I would go to university, but I only managed to get a C plus, which fell short of public university admission requirements," says the 29- year- old.

Never one to give up so easily, Ms. Mutai decided to press on, no matter the circumstances. "I came to Bomet Town and borrowed some *sukuma wiki* (kales), which I sold to a nearby restaurant at 100 percent profit," she says. "From there, many people started asking me to supply this or that. I saved every coin I got and used the money to source for contracts. I ended up supplying beans, millet, potatoes, carrots, bricks, and all manner of items," says Ms. Mutai.

She also plays a role in the livestock market by buying cows and sheep cheaply, then selling them during the high season when local farmers harvest maize or get tea bonuses. "People like me because I am reliable and I do my best to supply what I promise at whatever cost," she says.

This was the beginning of a business journey that culminated in her selection as one of the 14 finalists who flew to the University of Connecticut in the US for a two month young entrepreneurs' program sponsored by Techno serve and the US Government. Earlier, 6,000 young men and women had submitted business plans to the Ministry of Youth Affairs and Sports for a competition on the achievement of the Vision 2030.

Pocket Money

"My business plan won for giving blow-by- blow steps of how my village Muywek, which is on the border of Bomet and Sotik Districts, can be the first in the country to achieve Vision 2030," says the Sotik District Youth Leader.

"I thank God for this feat. From my business in supplies and construction, I have educated my five siblings through high school and college. This young entrepreneurs program will equip me in empowering the youth," the holder of two diplomas in Human Resource Management and Food and Nutrition told Money Magazine.

Her ambition is to build a Youth Empowerment Centre and a Sports Academy in Sotik. "The former has actually been realized as construction has started for a 12 million facility where youths of different talents can realize their dreams," says the astute businesswoman who is now worth more than 8 million.

Lessons
- Be patient; do not expect to get returns immediately.
- Customize your services to suit different kinds of clients.
- Diversify your range of services.
- From the story of Yaele Mutai you realize that it is not the size of the seed that determines the size of the tree but the size of faith and unending determination.

3. Avoid Total Dependence On Salary
(Adapted from The Standard Online Edition Posted on 28/11/2010 by John Kariuki)

If one is sacked, their social standing changes instantly from riches to rags. Some salaried employees often go through what can be described as a tragic cycle of saving, borrowing and repaying in a set number of years.

Granted that many people get employed while in their mid twenties, and that each cycle of saving, borrowing and repaying may take eight years, one can only make use of a maximum of four such cyclical loans in his or her working lifetime.

Often, the first loan is used to purchase a car or land, the second one for building a house or starting an income generating project. The third one, for tidying up all loose ends in ongoing projects that often include unfinished houses! Throw in school fees for children when on the second and third loans and you have a complex situation. The financial goals and priorities get a little muddled.

When taking the fourth such loan, some salaried people have many irons in the fire and they know well that this money will hardly solve any of them. And the ease with which financial institutions are hawking schemes such as, top-up, buy-out and mortgage and education loans on check-off basis, lures such borrowers with the possibility of starting all over again without their previous mistakes!

Comfort Zone
But this easy credit simply ensures that life is one continuous circus of borrowing and repaying, consequences of which spill into retirement. Content in their comfort zones, some professionals have no clue of how to get out of this yoke and think out of this box.

Their lives and financial destiny have been effectively sealed by a dependency on their pay slips and a stoppage of work for whatever reason would haul them into instant and often unmanageable debt and poverty! God forbid, but when such professionals are sacked, their apparent social standing changes instantly from riches to rags!

130

From flaunting swanky home entertainment systems, posh cars and expensive household items, and which are often bought on credit, such people frequently have nowhere to keep such conspicuous consumer goods, save for their ancestral homes in the rural areas! Their children, conditioned to live in the fast lane often become social misfits in their new environments.

According to Patrick Oluoch, a personal financial expert, the journey to financial freedom, for a salaried person starts with saving.
"It does not matter whether or not one earns sh10,000 or sh1 million a month, but if there is no deliberate saving effort, the money will always be insufficient to his or her monthly spending , deepening the dependence on salary," he says.

4. **The Earlier You Branch Out The Better It Is For Your Firm's Growth, adapted from Smart Company by J. Evans Nyabiage- jnyabiage@ke.nationmedia.com**
   (Source: Daily Nation December 20, 2010.)

The rich father says that people should be free from the proverbial rat race by going to school so that they can get big jobs with big salaries and even bigger expenses.

Every entrepreneur has his or her own success story but for Mr. Michael Macharia, the Chief Executive Officer of Seven Seas Technologies Ltd, this is nothing more than taking control of one's life at an appropriate time.

In 1995, into his first year at Egerton University he quit due to what he says was a course (Bachelor of Science) that he wasn't comfortable with. He was supposed to register for units in Mathematics, Physics and Chemistry. "I didn't like the course and had to discontinue my studies after a year. My parents were unhappy but I have no regrets. I took control of my life at 20," he told Smart Company in an interview.

Just like Mr. Macharia's story, in his book, "Rich Dad, Poor Dad," Robert Kiyosaki had two fathers. The real father is an educated professor who schooled at Harvard but died very poor while the other, his mentor dropped out of school but became one of the richest men in Hawaii.

The rich father says people should free themselves from the proverbial rat race – going to school so that they complete and get big jobs with big salaries and even bigger expenses. Kiyosaki says one should spot opportunities and create solutions so that they make money work for them and not working for money.

The book, aside, after Egerton, Mr. Macharia went to pursue accounting courses (CPA). He says that the reason why many entrepreneurs fail to succeed is because they take long to make decisions. "Why should someone wait to be 30 years to start a business?" he asks, adding that most people cling on what he terms as 'safety nets' such as a degree, a good paying job, name of a company, their parents, and in the end fail to do what they should have done while young.

At the age of 21, he worked for his first and only employer for three years, Comtech Systems (a former IT company owned by the Aga Khan Development Network), where he joined as an accounting intern and eventually held the role of Finance Manager. Dr. Wahome Gakuru, a lecturer in Strategy and Entrepreneurship says there is massive disconnect in political governance, to a big extend hurting many entrepreneurs in Kenya.

Pocket Money

Dr. Gakuru who was one of the front men in drafting vision 2030, sums the challenges facing entrepreneurs in Kenya especially start-ups and small and medium enterprises (SMEs) into four; lack of an enabling policy environment, access to capital, particularly disturbing – the fight for talent or human capital and governance and succession planning.

Mr. Macharia, in what he calls a blueprint on how to run an ICT company outlines the following as encounters for successful entrepreneurs – brand positioning, capital, people, regional expansion, vision, innovation, corporate governance, focus, and partnerships. Others are systems and processes and finally mentorship. He says that establishing a strong brand starts while at first jobs or assignments and the people one interacts with.

After he quit Comtech, he secured his first contract with Rwanda Government, although there were a myriad of problems. First, he had no major firm and second there were no qualified engineers to carry out the job at the time. The first engineer he sourced from Kenya did a shoddy job and he had to get another from India. On completion of the assignment he made $ 150,000 (Sh12 million at the current exchange rate).

"This was the birth of seven Seas Technologies. "In 2,000, this amount was a lot but I used it wisely," he says. Currently, the firm has annual top-line revenue of about Shs2 billion employing more than 80 engineers.

Ms. Radhika Lee, the founder of Nairobi International School, says one of the challenges that new entrepreneurs face is the change of mind-set – from being staff to owning an enterprise. And when one enters the market, she says, one is met with stiff competition with already established businesses. "We are in competition with acres and acres of schools. We must have something unique to stand out," Ms. Lee said, at a recent entrepreneurship workshop.

While appreciating that Kenya entrepreneurs have great ideas with more young talents waiting to be nurtured, Mr Macharia says access to capital remains a major constraint.

Mr. Ayisi Makatiani, the Managing Partner and CEO of Fanisi Capital Ltd, which manages the Fanisi Venture Capital Fund, says start-ups and SMEs, usually in need of up to sh240 million ($3 million) are the most difficult area to invest. He says owners of ventures in ICT, and agribusiness are good in technical aspects but poor at expanding.

Some years into business Mr. Macharia attracted a venture capitalist who invested into the company. Recently the firm secured private equity funding of sh400 million ($5 million from Aureos capital a Global Private equity Fund.

"One of the challenges we face as entrepreneurs is the acceptance of your own product in the market. The other challenge is the time it takes to be accepted as a successful entrepreneur," Mr. Macharia observes.

He says between the fourth and seventh year into business, it is near death and those that survive start gaining recognition after the eighth year and thereafter market dominance.

Few Role Models
Then there are also historical challenges.
According to Mr. Macharia, there are not enough role models in the market or there is little or no effort given by the media to showcase such success stories. The entrepreneurs also need to make an effort to showcase their successes.

Mr. Jimnah Mbaru, an investment banker and owner of Dyer and Blair Investment Bank, said at a workshop that in many cases pioneers in the market do not make money, but act like John the Baptist.

"For me starting a business is the easy part, but transforming it to a professional management is the hard part," he says. This, he says is the biggest challenge for many entrepreneurs who do not want to micro- manage everything. "It is good at some point to spur growth of the business to give professional management to run the business," he adds.

"It is entirely on you to have self governance. You do not have to wait; it should be natural. The interest to change must start from within," says Mr. Sunny Bindra, a Nairobi based management consultant.

5. **At 27, She Already Owns Lodge At The Maasai Mara**
   (Adapted from Daily Nation on the web by Julius Sigei, 22nd Dec..2010.)
Sylvia Ntutu has turned her late father's historical home into a guest house, and is beginning to reap dividends. When in 2007 she told her family that she was starting a tourist resort in the world famous Maasai Mara Game Reserve, Sylvia Ntutu Kuluo, then only 24, was told she was crazy and that her idea would come to nothing.

"I had just completed a Public Relations course at the Nairobi Institute of Business Studies and they thought that what I needed most was a job as I did not have a cent," she told Money Magazine at her scenic Kileleoni Mara Guest House and Camp, on the north eastern edge of the reserve.

"I reluctantly took up a job at Fairmont Mara Safari Club, where I gained experience running a tourist class hotel. I also saved money and laid strategies for my eventual take-off," says the mother of one, adding that her dream finally came true when she was granted permission to renovate her late father's seven-bed-room house.

The legendary paramount chief Lerionka Ntutu had 10 wives and 63 children. "I thank God because out of all my siblings, it is I, the last born daughter, who has let this home live on," she says, adding that she intends to make the house a heritage as it is an attraction in itself.

After getting the go-ahead she convinced her husband, Nicholas Karino Kuluo, to plunge their scarce resources into renovating it. "Once Nick accepted, I never looked back and he has been central in the success of our firm," she says.

The couple pooled its resources, bought a Land Rover to help in transportation of materials, and took a Ksh500, 000 loan from Equity Bank. "But the renovation has not been easy. At one point, thieves stole our conduit pipes and when we bought others, they were crushed by elephants," says Mr. Kuluo.

But as things became "elephant," so did their determination grow. "I could not imagine letting the dream die. We went back to the bank and thankfully, it believed in us and loaned us more money," says Mrs. Kuluo, adding that they had, in the meantime, supplemented their earnings by supplying fresh vegetables and fruits to lodges in the reserve.

"Our efforts were crowned when we won a competitive tender to host the first-ever Maasai Mara Marathon last year and we have just concluded one this year," says Mr. Kuluo on their web site. The extravaganza attracted more than 1,000 guest house and tents. They netted sh1 million in one night and have now trained their eyes on a luxury camp with 14 tents. "It will be ready in time for the Christmas season and we already have bookings lined up," Mrs. Kuluo chips in.

Lessons
• Never let anyone bring you down. Be focused and believe in yourself.
• Do not over-consult. Talk to only two or three trusted friends and experts. This will reduce the number of people bound to discourage you.
• Do not focus on the profits first. Currently we are repaying loans and improving our facility.

6. Message From The Chairman Mr. Titus K. Muya
(Adapted from www.familybank.co.ke)

The history of this bank started earlier than 1984. It started when the dream for starting a bank occurred to me way back in the early 1960s when I was a young man in High School. I lived with this dream through the 1960s to 1981 when I started visiting the Treasury looking for a license to start a bank.

We started our operations in November 1984 by renting an office along Kenyatta Avenue. We could not open a full branch in Nairobi as we found the rent too high. We therefore moved to Kiambu where it was cheaper. We opened our first branch in 1985 and by the year 2000 we had opened 10 branches.

At this juncture, the business was growing, the branches were increasing and the customer numbers were growing. Due to our limited resources we decided to focus on doing business with the lower end of the market. We also noted that the mainstream banks were deserting this market. So we came up with suitable loan products for them.

The other reason customers came to us is because at that time both the local and foreign mainstream banks were deserting this market and had become very insensitive to their customers needs and feelings. We at Family saw an opportunity in this behaviour which we decided to exploit. With all these efforts the Kenyans could not and did not disappoint us. The Kenyans received us very warmly every province we went to.

With this support we grew in all parameters; loans, customer numbers, assets, deposits, and even capital. Our strategy team later found out that as a building society we could sell shares to our customers and staff through private placements. Consequent upon this some 7000 customers and staff injected some Ksh700 million as new capital. This capital helped to seamlessly convert from a building society to a fully fledged commercial bank in 2007.

After conversion we experienced even faster growth. With this growth more capital was needed. We agreed on another rights issue and the balance of the unsold shares was offered to the foreign bidders. We talked to a few potential foreign investors and selected one with whom we embarked on negotiations. In the end we reached an agreement.

The partnership we have launched today will not only increase our capital to, over Kshs.3B but will also boost our liquidity and boost our deposit taking capacity to over Kshs.40Billion. This investment will create an appetite for expanding to the region and start planning on listing at the Nairobi Stock Exchange.

Our new profile now stands as follows; we are currently the 5th largest in customer numbers and branch network. We are rated as a Tier One Bank meaning we are now playing at the national league of the ten or so largest banks in the country.

7. Tricks Children Use To Skim Cash Off You
(Source: Daily nation of Thursday December 30, 2010.)

Some parents box themselves into a corner by setting up a culture of conspicuous consumption in their children which may dog them in employment and later life. With the new school year kicking off next Monday, many parents will fail for the many tricks employed by teenagers in obtaining more money than they need.

And the tragedy is that in their enthusiasm, some parents shower their children with excess money for use in school.
They box themselves into a corner by setting up a culture of conspicuous consumption in their children, a mistake that can dog them in employment and later life.

There have been extreme cases in secondary school where some parents give their children as much as sh13, 000 per term or Ksh1, 300 every week for their "personal use." This translates to Ksh39, 000 per year and Ksh159, 000 over the entire four year course. This money could buy a modest stake in the stock market, doubling or tripling in four years to give you a fabulous return.

Often, such children end up with disciplinary issues in school. They may try out drugs, alcohol and play truant. Often, they pay other less privileged students to do their washing, homework and assigned duties for them, besides running errands to obtain contraband.

Besides growing up with the wrong notion that money can buy practically anything, including friendship, such pampered children fail to get the all important lesson of financial prudence at a critical and impressionable age.

So, the question is how much money is enough to leave with your child in school? While you need to ask around from other seasoned parents or teachers on the acceptable cash to entrust a child in a particular school, pocket money not exceeding Ksh.2, 000 is fine.

In addition to this, factor in expenses like the bus fare back home on closing day, over-the-counter medication, occasional refreshments when on school outings and emergencies like loss of some clothes and so on. But our youth are not altogether dumb; they devise new schemes to defraud their parents. Some students' money-getting designs include soliciting for funds to pay for up-coming school trips and a dramatization of set books and so on.

As a parent, verify all these activities with the school authorities and, more importantly, the amount required.
Often, the charges are upped generously to leave the student a little stipend. There is a problem if your child has suddenly become outgoing with so many trips in a term. This is often a pointer to a spendthrift lifestyle that could be unsustainable, given your resources and overheads of school fees.

A student desperate for cash will often fake a misfortune, like theft of all his or her personal effects. He or she will claim to have borrowed heavily from friends and to request you the parent or guardian to foot the bill. It may all look perfect and sensible, until you examine the nitty-gritty. Everything is likely to be overpriced and you can easily do a physical check on the items purported to have been bought to verify their newness.

When your child asks for extra cash to cater for a special diet in school, be afraid and get to the bottom of the problem quickly. Demand to see the note of whoever gave this prescription and verify it with him or her. Ask why the problem has suddenly arisen in school and it is never there at home. As often happens, our youth exaggerate simple medical issues with a calculated financial aim in mind.

It is a mark of maturity for your child to buy all his or her things. But many parents are often hoodwinked that some things are so expensive nowadays and only available in obscure shops where the children do their back-to-school shopping. If this has been happening to you, your child could be making a generous saving and using the extra money for other things.

Also keep a tab on the lies your extended kin are getting from your child and the kind of money they are parting with.

Secondary school students often learn of who has a soft spot for them and capitalize on it with all sorts of woeful tales calculated to earning them sympathy and some cash.

One way of making your children allies in your financial journey is to let them earn their pocket money. They can help you in your business over the school holidays for a fee. This way, they are likely to understand the value of money and prudence in its spending.

Let your secondary school children learn of your house and business premises rents, power and water bills and other overheads. Indeed, sending them occasionally to pay some of these bills may give them a sense of your expenditure vis-à-vis their demands.

8. Well Rounded Students Who Can Think Are Lacking.

A KCPE Report By Wachira Kigotho (Adapted from groups.yahoo.com/group/outofafricamessages /322 on 9/12/2010)

A 2010 online poll dubbed, "Raise Your Hand," generated over 325 ideas from students, parents, teachers, higher education and early learning specialists. But five ideas stood out.

At the top of the list was the idea that schools must become forums where students are taught how to think and not just to regurgitate textbook facts. There was general consensus that education should be a public good and responsibility. Gaining popularity was the idea that schooling should focus more on creating long-term love for learning and ability to think critically rather than teaching to pass examinations.

In forth position was the idea that all children should have opportunities to discover their natural abilities and be provided with facilities to develop them. Most participants urged governments and other stakeholders in education to ensure children from disadvantaged backgrounds have the same opportunity to quality education as others.

The five priorities are reflection that schools in most countries have failed to teach basic competencies that would enable students to acquire vital skills. According to Tamar Manuelyan Atinc, the Vice President of the World Bank's Human Development Network, many children are in school but are not learning anything of value.

In a recent report, stepping up skills: for more jobs and Higher productivity, Atinc says, "Learning outcomes indicate schools in most developing countries are not providing students with basic skills that make them trainable for the labour market." The report that has been prepared by a team of education and labour experts at the World Bank is critical of most education systems in Sub-Saharan Africa where there is a backlog of pupils performing poorly. "The message is fix it," says the report.

Quoting early grade assessment reports on Kenya among other countries in the sub-region, the report says large numbers of students do not achieve minimum levels of learning expected. "Low proportions of pupils can read simple sentences with ease and comprehension, making it harder for those pupils to catch up later," says the report.

Basically, stepping up skills takes off from where Raise Your Hand poll stopped. It highlights how countries should provide occupational skills to their youth and pinpoints out how constraints of skills have been a barrier to employment.

"Skills constraints are one reason of low productivity and earnings in Sub-Saharan Africa where population growth outpaces new jobs," says the report.

"For instance in Kenya, Ethiopia, Rwanda and Uganda, inadequacy in a range of skills – technical, scientific, entrepreneurial and managerial – has reduced potential for pursuing new opportunities in bio-fuels, medicinal plants and green technology," says the report.

Technology Ladder
But the report warns the situation is likely to worsen unless schools start preparing students for training in job-relevant skills. Quoting recent enterprise surveys undertaken by the World Bank, the report says complaints about skills are voiced by newer firms that are eager to move up the technology ladder.

Apart from those elementary competencies, schools have also to provide skills that are directed for workplace. According to Ms. Elizabeth King, who was one of the authors of the report, most youths leaving schooling in sub-Saharan Africa have no problem-solving, learning, communication, personal and social skills. They include basic skills in physical sciences, mathematics and social sciences. Besides, they also require skills for tasks to be performed in workplace – accuracy, timeliness, commitment to quality, performance and value of work are mandatory. "Unless those skills are taught, most youths in urban areas in Sub-Saharan Africa will continue to make a living in low-skilled jobs," says King.

But whereas, it is understandable that relevant job skills are crucial to employment and self-entrepreneurial enterprise, most school systems have failed to improve learning. In tatters are building blocks of schooling that encompassing learning standards, good teachers, adequate resources and proper regulatory systems.

9. My MBA Isn't Helping My Career
By Suzanne Lucas (Adapted from evilhrlady.org/2010/10/my-mba-isnt-helping-my-career.html)

Dear Evil HR Lady,
"About a year ago I finished my MBA. While working on my MBA, I had imagined that there would be plenty of opportunities when I graduated. Unfortunately even with an advanced degree, my two years in finance are not enough to qualify me for advanced positions.
My current employer gave me a great retention bonus, yet no raise. Senior management told me that I do an outstanding job, and that they do not want to lose me. My current salary is only a couple of thousand dollars more than when I started with the company and is significantly less than what my current position was advertised for.
I get the bonus in December and am not sure that they are going to offer me the salary I have in mind. I am wondering if you can give me some tips for negotiating. Also should I be looking at other jobs so that I have firm counter offers to come back to them with? My student loans are all due and I cannot afford to pay those and pay all of my other monthly bills like my mortgage and car payment."

Pocket Money

This is a proof that the testimonials we use to show what we are worth may not reflect our capability, our productivity and our pay. Going to school so that we can get more good grades with an eye on positions and pay may come but still twisted. When employed you hold the short end of the stick no matter the amount of money you earn. Your creativity in the company is limited. Your good ideas may be trampled on. This is the very reason why one should be able to know why they are in school.

10. Young Marketer Catches Global Eye
   (Adapted from the Standard Saturday Magazine Instinct of 08/05/2010)

Beatrice Ndung'u started her online magazine at 21 after dropping out of college due to lack of fees. Today, at 24, the Kenya Youth Ambassador is the CEO of Global Essence, a marketing and advertising firm, writes Joan Barsulai.

At only 21 years, when most people merely think about good grades, Beatrice Ndung'u had already started her own online marketing company. By 22, she had bought her first car and, now at 24, Beatrice has carved a niche for herself as the CEO of a successful and wide reaching marketing company- Global Essence. Not only is her company serving local clientele, but it is also reaching the East, Central and Southern Africa, as well as the diaspora.

Life has however not always been rosy for Beatrice. She had to drop out of college, at Nairobi Institute of Business Studies, in 2007 after her father retired from his job at the UN and had no money to continue paying her school fees. Even so, Beatrice has always had a kin interest in the media, and while at home, she wrote several articles, and from this she birthed the concept of an online magazine.

Within two weeks, she had the concept ready and she presented it to her pleasantly surprised parents, who thought she should definitely take it further. She was cash strapped, so her father decided to contact a friend of his in Belgium, who agreed to sponsor the magazine, after he saw the impressive designs.

Help From Odinga
That same year, Beatrice launched the online magazine *globalesseence.net*. The publication has now got as many as 100,000 hits monthly. But she was not satisfied with the results, so she reworked the magazine and gave it a much better outlook.

In 2008, she re-launched it with its new look, but she realized she was short of funds to enable her to run it efficiently. She was desperately in need of a capital injection and an office.
After unsuccessfully asking around for funds, she decided to take a bold step – she got the number of Fidel Odinga, Prime Minister Raila Odinga's son, from a friend, and decided to call him. Says Beatrice: "I had never met him before, and I was very afraid of what the outcome would be, but I was desperate and I had no other options." She called him and introduced herself, and explained what she was doing. He was so astounded by her initiative and ambition, given her age that he wrote her a cheque, which she used to buy computers and rent office space. With funds at hand she now started marketing her business fully.

Undeterred, she attended several social functions, where she handed out her business cards to VIPs. One client that she was eyeing, PLO Lumumba, was impressed by her determination and focus, being such a young girl, and he even offered her a job, which she had to turn down because she was trying to get her own business off the ground.

146

Today, Global Essence has expanded to include a creative department, an online magazine as well as production department, which runs its media unit, R&B, tasked with creating ads for various companies. The advertisements have been so successful, that Beatrice confesses to being overwhelmed.

Her ever-expanding company has created several employment opportunities for people countrywide, including freelance writers, and managers who are running the R&B Media Department.

She feels so lucky that she encourages the youth everywhere to e-mail her their success stories, which publishes on her online magazine often. "Many people think that women cannot get far. But all you have to take is the initiate. Be determined and ambitious; know what you want and do not apologize for it. Everyone can do something – the difference is that some people take the initiative and others don't," she says.

Beatrice's life has never been the same, since making it big. She is now a role model for so many girls, who come to her for advice on everything. She enjoys mentoring young people in business.

Beatrice At A Glance

Started an online magazine at 21, is now 24 and the CEO of Global Essence, a marketing firm. Is the second born in a family of three. Has been appointed the Kenya Youth Ambassador by All Eyes on Africa: Dare to Dream, a group for Kenyans in the Diaspora. Dropped out of college in 2007 due to lack of fees.

She explains, "I always just walk up to young people who seem to have lost their way, especially the ones who idle around in the estate and abuse drugs, and I speak to them. I cannot let someone waste away – not on my watch, and not if I can do something about it."

This year, Beatrice was awarded the Kenya Youth Ambassador by a group of Kenyans living in the Diaspora. The group named All Eyes on Africa: Dare to Dream, which is nurturing young people, decided that Beatrice deserved the title, after hearing about all her achievements at such a tender age.

She says she has also achieved international success; she was recently interviewed on a US radio station, Blogtalk Radio, along with Martin Luther King Jr, where she spoke about her business venture and the potential of African youth. The station appointed her their youth ambassador in Kenya.

That is not the only accolade under Beatrice's belt. She was also declared the best speaker by the Rotary Club, Kenya, after giving a speech at the Rotary Club in Hurlingham. In that speech she shared her experience as an entrepreneur and her future plans for the youth. She has also been profiled in several websites based in the US, as well as in local radio and television stations.

And the hits keep coming. She was recently hired by Royal Media Services to run all creative works for Citizen Television. In an informal survey on facebook, Beatrice was named the 6th top media socialite in the country. She attributes her great success to her family, without which she says she would never have been who she is today.

The second born in a family of three children, her financial success could not have come at a better time – her father has recently retired and she is now the breadwinner of the family. Her older sister, Caroline Roza, who lives in the UK, is the Global Essence Marketing Manager abroad.

Pocket Money

Beatrice is also thankful for her creative streak, which she says she relies on in her day to day work. "I am creative – I work quickly and have a wealth of ideas to choose from," says the prodigy. When not busy, Beatrice likes to unwind by reading comic books or playing the piano.

She continues to climb the ladder of success, with businessmen from around the world requesting to partner with her. She is currently in partnership with business moguls from South Africa, with whom she plans to start a new business venture later this year.

Beatrice plans to expand her creative and production department, with the help of several business partnerships she has been receiving. She notes, "I want to have the best marketing company in the country, and give Gina Din and Scanad a run for their money."

Asserting her faith in the ability to achieve the impossible, Beatrice says that the next 10 years hold a lot of promise for her. She intends to play on the global stage and be successful beyond her wildest dreams.

Chapter 13

TRACKING YOUR POCKET MONEY

Pocket Money

It is a common practice to spend our monies as stipulated in the previous chapter. I alluded that what we earn is subdivided in different ways through paying bills, purchasing food, paying taxes, offering alms and saving the rest. At any level we spend and we lose the purchasing power by gaining the value worth our money. Most of the transactions are sealed by the presentation of a receipt. A receipt is a written acknowledgement of having received an item of a specific value. It mainly has an outline of the purchase, the date of purchase, the value of the purchase and more information from the seller. A transaction receipt is your proof of a completed transaction.

Apparently, not all transactions have a receipt accompanying them. Despite the vital role played by these small pieces of paper few people or small businesses keep them unless it is required by a superior or a vote holder in an organization. Transaction receipts play a number of roles namely:

1. Accountability- receipts indicate and show accountability for amount spend and for what purpose and time of transaction. In organizations when a person is responsible over some money the proof of expenditure is a valid receipt. For personal finances it should also indicate you spend your money on a valuable good or source. A valid receipt is one that has stamp of the origin company or a logo or name of the origin organization. Many a times we get receipts and throw them away. We do not keep them. This is evident in supermarkets bins, ATM machine room's, bank bins and on the streets. In fact if we kept and used the receipts for their purpose we could rid our environment litter.

2. Launching complaints- once you realize the balance or the worth of purchased item or excess deductions or additions are faulty, you can use the receipts in launching a complaint to the receipt originator. Without the proof of a receipt then no one would believe you transacted with them even if they saw you.

3. **Tracking finances-** receipts are a simple way to track individual organizational finances. Auditors in companies request for receipts to track how a company or organization finances were spend. This way companies are able to be accountable to its shareholders, donors, workers and managers.

At the individual level it should do the same. One should keep all receipts for transactions for every particular month. For transactions which are un-receipted one can get a home receipt book on which they will be indicating the transactions then keep the receipts.

Commonly Un-Receipted Transactions Include

1. **Religious contributions-** these are contributions made in religious precincts. A number of these contributions are not acknowledged by issuance of a receipt.

2. **Charitable contributions-** these include money you give to beggars on the streets, and in the villages and in *harambee*.

3. **Money gifts-** money one dishes out as a gift to someone. For example during baby shower events, weddings or money you give someone as lunch or breakfast.

4. **Petty cash lending-** sometimes people lend each other small amounts of money which one forgets and never receive back. For instance a friend asks for twenty, fifty or hundred shillings when you are on the street or in a vehicle. Some of these monies are not returned and you may not ask either but they represent a minus from your side which you should account for.

5. *Transport costs*- most commuter vehicles do not provide receipts for short distances. The monies we spend on transport with no receipt are likely not to be accounted for.

6. *Street purchases*- many a times we notice something unplanned for on the streets and buy it. These may include pens, books, compact disks, skirts, shirts socks, or even have our nails polished. Normally these purchases are not receipted. What is bought may be consumed immediately meaning the transaction is forgotten. This may spell doom when accounting for ones salary and pocket money at the end of the day.

7. *Street meals*- these are meals we purchase while on transit whether on foot or on by a vehicle. Generally one would purchase a fruit salad, sweets, biscuits, chewing gum, roasted maize and some *mutura*.

8. *Saloon and kinyozi services*- after a haircut or a hair tending normally we pay and walk out. This spending requires to be accounted for.

9. *Grocer goods*- the grocer sales vegetables and other lean packaged goods and services. These are services we spend on daily but we may not be recording them. For those with house helps we can help them in doing the recording for each month.

10.   *Money we give to friends and family members*- as a grown-up with parents, siblings, grandparents and relatives it is African to give these groups of people some money as pocket money. We normally would give but do not ask for a receipt. These are our expenses which we can account for through a recording book or receipting.

11.   *Shop or store transactions*- when dealing with kadogo economy in small shops and sheds, proof of transaction is not provided inform of a receipt.

12.   *Call girl/boy services*- after a good time with a call girl or call boy you pay them but they do not provide receipts for their services. This is an expenditure to which one should be able to account for.

These are some of the common transactions we encounter on daily basis that after we have spent, we remain with no proof of the transaction unless we record somewhere. Most of these un-intended, un-receipted and un-unrecorded costs escape our mind and we may lose our finances by not tracking them.

The Bible in Songs of Solomon tells us that young foxes destroy the vines. It is these small expenditures that ruin the bigger plans. They derail plans by reducing the overall ability to implement the intended plans.

Common Receipted Transactions Include:
1. *Supermarket transactions-* supermarkets provide a detailed transaction receipt. Mostly it shows a lot of details including date, cost and description of transaction and the supermarket details including the person who served you.
2. *Bank transactions-* after an over the counter transaction banks provide a receipt which you as the customer have to sign. Automated teller machines always ask a person whether they require a receipt. Bank transaction receipts show bank details, date of transaction, account details bank branch and sometimes the reason or nature of transaction.
3. *Learning institutions-* they provide receipts for transactions done with them as proof.
4. *Some church contributions-* some churches provide receipts for transactions like tithe and first produce.
5. *Long distance travel and courier services-* courier and human transport are receipted to show evidence of transaction with the particular company.

6. Book store- bookshops; provide receipts as proof of transactions made with them.

7. Mobile transactions- when we use mobile money transfer services we usually receive confirmation messages as proof of the transaction.

8. Hotel and restaurant transaction- they provide receipts for the transaction detailing conditions of occupation or meals consumed.

9. Online transactions- online payments through credit cards also get receipt which one should print and keep.

10. Fuel and gas stations- fueling stations provide receipts for their transactions.

With some transactions being receipted and others not being receipted, what is the big idea? It is possible to track your monthly finances despite all this. Parents can train their children on how to be responsible with money through budgeting, shopping lists and tracking their expenses. The tracking can be done using receipts and recordings. There are a number of things one can do to enhance their efficiency and accountability with pocket money or other finances.

1. Keep receipts- for all receipted transactions the receipt should be kept. If the receipt lacks part of the information you want on it you should inscribe the information on it. If possible indicate the reason of the purchase.

2. Ask for a receipt- in some shops or stores the attendants refrain from issuing a receipt in transactions to evade paying some accruing taxes. If you know that a certain transaction should be receipted then insist on a receipt. In some cases the seller may ask you to pay more for the receipted item. With a receipt if what is bought is defective then you can return it and get a replacement, but with no receipt you can only bank on the good will of the seller.

3. *Have own receipt book*- a number of un-receipted transactions have been highlighted which sometimes are difficult to be receipted. To account for this expenditures one can purchase their own receipt themselves. For example after buying vegetables or having your shoes polished you write the date, activity, cost and reason of expenditure.

This own receipting will serve to gap all areas of expenditure which are effected but not receipted anywhere. For school going children the same applies. If you purchase a book a toast, tooth paste or a snack. Indicate somewhere or write in your own receipt and then keep the receipt.

4. *Keep a recording book*- alternatively you can buy a book and divide it in a number of columns to be recording all transactions. Ensure the columns capture the date, unit cost, total cost and reason of transaction. Also include the supplier or service provider. Complete this book daily. If you're busy assign this to the house help then monitor.

5. *Keep all ATM receipts*- you walk in an ATM machine room and you find many ATM transaction receipts lying on the floor. Many people do not keep them. It is advisable to keep these receipts. To track the finances one should indicate the reason for the transaction. For example, "Withdrew 10,000 to buy a printer or withdrew 5,000 to buy a drink."

6. *Soft copy receipt*- these are mobile information messages and credit card transaction and e-mail receipts. It is advisable to print and file these soft copy receipts for reference purposes.

In addition you can also record those transactions in your recording book. This is because mobile messages can be deleted and e-mail accounts can crush. It is possible to retrieve the lost information but can cost time and more money.

7. *Match budget, shopping list with monthly tracked transactions*- do your monthly calculations and compare them with budgeted items for the month. Doing this from month to month enables you to isolate money wasting routes and gap them in successive months. This is a simple way to track finances and setting the stage to financial freedom.

8. Using a receipt or a recording book you are able to identify unintentional purchases, or point of impulse buying- at the end of the day the amount spent should be accounted for.

9. Use a finance tracking software- there are financial software's which one can buy and be keying in the entries on daily basis.

Conclusion

A story is told of a young academically excellent man who applied for a managerial position in a big company. He passed the first interview but the director who did the last interview had the final word.

The director discovered from the CV that the youth's academic achievements were excellent all the way, from secondary school until the postgraduate research, never had a year passed without him scoring.

The director asked, "Did you obtain any scholarships in school?" The youth answered, "None."

The director asked, "Was it your father who paid for your school fees?" The youth answered, "My father passed away when I was one year old, it was my mother who paid for my school fees." The director asked, "Where did your mother work?" The youth answered, "My mother worked as clothes cleaner." The director requested the youth to show his hands. The youth showed a pair of hands that were smooth and perfect.

The director asked, "Have you ever helped your mother wash the clothes before?" The youth answered, "Never, my mother always wanted me to study and read more books. Furthermore, my mother can wash clothes faster than me." The director said, "I have a request. When you go back today, go and clean your mother's hands, and then see me tomorrow morning."

Pocket Money

The youth felt that his chance of landing the job was high. When he went back, he happily requested his mother to let him clean her hands. His mother felt strange, happy but with mixed feelings, she showed her hands to the kid.

The youth cleaned his mother's hands slowly. Tears fell down his face as he washed her hands. For the first time he noticed that his mother's hands were wrinkled and had many bruises. Some were so painful that his mother shivered as he cleaned them.

In many years, the young man realized that it was this pair of hands that washed the clothes everyday to enable him to pay the school fees. The bruises in his mother's hands were the price that she had to pay for his graduation, academic excellence and his future.

After he was done cleaning his mother's hand, the young man quietly washed all the remaining clothes.

That night, mother and son talked for a long time. The next morning, the he went to the director's office. The Director noticed the tears in his eyes and asked, "Can you tell me what you did and learned yesterday in your house?"

The young man answered, "I cleaned my mother's hands, and also finished cleaning all the remaining clothes." The Director asked, "Please tell me your feelings."

The youth said, "Number 1, I know now what appreciation is. Without my mother, there would not be the successful me today. Number 2, by working together and helping my mother, I now realize how difficult and tough it is to get something done. Number 3, I have come to appreciate the importance and value of family relationship."

The Director said, "This is what I am looking for to be my manager. I want to recruit a person who can appreciate the help of others, a person who knows the sufferings of others to get things done, and a person who would not put money as his only goal in life. You are hired."

Later on, this young man worked hard, and received the respect of his subordinates. All employees worked diligently and as a team. The company's performance improved tremendously.

A child, who has been protected and habitually given whatever he wanted, would develop "entitlement mentality" and would always put himself first. He would be ignorant of his parent's efforts. When he starts work, he assumes that every person must listen to him, and when he becomes a manager, he would never know the sufferings of his employees and would always blame others. For this kind of people, who may be good academically, may be successful for a while, but eventually would not feel sense of achievement. He will grumble and be full of hatred and fight for more. If we are this kind of protective parents, are we really showing love or are we destroying the kid instead?

You can let your kid live in a big house, eat a good meal, learn piano, watch a big screen TV. But when you are cutting grass, please let them experience it. After a meal, let them wash their plates and bowls together with their brothers and sisters. It is not because you do not have money to hire a maid, but it is because you want to love them in a right way. You want them to understand, no matter how rich their parents are, one day their hair will grow gray, same as the mother of that young person. The most important thing is your kid learns how to appreciate the effort and experience the difficulty and learns the ability to work with others to get things done.

160

I believe that, through these letters of the English alphabet and the numbered white papers, we have met Not because we are related but because we are connected. If you find the content of this book helpful, extend the connection forward by giving a copy to someone.

Also, extend the connection backwards by dropping an email to the address below about your take on the book.

For inspirational talks, seminars, conferences, key note address and mentoring programs kindly contact us on

+254721137478

matatamuthoka@gmail.com
pockettymoney@gmail.com